T0161987

100 TOP TIPS

Microsoft

Excel

- ◔ **Supercharge your Excel skills**
- ◔ **Learn more from your data**
- ◔ **Boost your productivity**

in easy steps

In easy steps is an imprint of In Easy Steps Limited
16 Hamilton Terrace · Holly Walk · Leamington Spa
Warwickshire · United Kingdom · CV32 4LY
www.ineasysteps.com

Notice of Liability
Every effort has been made to ensure that this book contains accurate and
current information. However, In Easy Steps Limited and the author shall
not be liable for any loss or damage suffered by readers as a result of any
information contained herein.

Trademarks
All trademarks are acknowledged as belonging to their respective
companies.

In Easy Steps Limited supports The Forest Stewardship Council (FSC), the
leading international forest certification organization. All our titles that are
printed on Greenpeace approved FSC certified paper carry the FSC logo.

MIX
Paper from
responsible sources
FSC® C020837

Printed and bound in the United Kingdom

ISBN 978-1-84078-879-2

ontents

3

100 TOP TIPS

ntering data with Auto Fill

ou're typing in data that has a pattern to it, Excel can
mplete the pattern for you. You can use this for number
quences, times, and dates.

1 Enter the start of the sequence into two cells. If it's
a number sequence, you'll need to enter at least
two numbers. For times and dates, Excel can use
just one. For alternate months (January, March,
etc.), you'd enter the first two to show the pattern.

2 Highlight the cells containing your data.

3 Click the Fill handle. It's a tiny
dot in the bottom right of
the selected area. Your cursor
becomes a small black cross
when you hover over it.

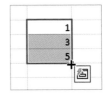

4 Drag the mouse to cover
the area you want to fill. In
the example shown here, you'd drag down. As
you drag, you'll see the value that's being added
shown next to your cursor.

5 Click the Auto Fill Options menu that appears
beside your cursor to find options for the fill,
including Copy, which fills each cell with the data
you've selected. You can also fill weekdays, days,
months, or years from dates. Try putting 31-Jan
in the first box, then autofilling months to get the
last day of each month.

5 Even quicker: If you just want a sequence of
numbers going up by 1, enter the first number,
select the cell and hold down Ctrl while you drag
the Fill handle.

Filling to matc
the neighboring colum

There's an even quicker way to autofill a range so it match
the size of the neighboring columns.

1 Enter the first two data items in the sequence yo
want to use. For example, if you want to add yea
starting at 2025 and want to increase by 1 each
time, enter 2025 and 2026 into two cells.

2 Highlight both cells containing the data items yo
just entered.

Period	US sales	UK sales
2025	65	11
2026	72	22
	46	232
	98	12
	23	54
		45
		54

3 Double-click the Fill handle in the bottom right o
the selected area.

4 Your data column is
automatically filled
to match the size
of the neighboring
columns. In my
example, the
autofill extends to
where the data
ends in the third
column, even
though the nearest
column is shorter.

Period	US sales	UK sales
2025	65	11
2026	72	22
2027	46	232
2028	98	12
2029	23	54
2030		45
2031		54

roduced in Excel 2013, Flash Fill recognizes patterns
data based on neighboring cells. It's much more
phisticated than Auto Fill. You can use it, for example, to
ormat text and split or combine data. Here's an example.

You might have a list of names, with the first name
and last name combined. For the first row, type the
first and second names into the next cells. This is
how you teach Excel the pattern to copy.

Name	First Name	Surname
Murphy Slaw	Murphy	Slaw
Bob Sled		
Phil Space		
Dave Triffids		
Gladys Working		

Position your cursor in the empty first name cell for
the second name.

Press Ctrl + E or click the Flash Fill button on
the ribbon. Find it by clicking the Data tab, then
looking in the Data Tools.

The first name column is then automatically filled
out for you. Check the results look okay, and then
do the same for the last name column.

Here are some tips for adjusting the width of columns. Similar ideas apply to rows.

1 To adjust the width of a column, click and drag the line to the right of its letter above the colum Here, I'm adjusting the width of column C.

◢	A	B	C ↔	D	E	F
1						

2 To make the column width snap to the width of the content in the column, double-click this sam dividing line above the column, on its right.

3 You can select several columns and adjust them at the same time, making them equal width, or making them all snap to their content width. To select a column, click its letter. Click and drag on the letters to select multiple columns, or use Ctrl click to select columns that aren't adjacent.

4 You might want to set the column width to a particular cell in the column, rather than the wid cell. Perhaps one cell contains a title that you're happy to run into other cells. Select the cell you want to adjust the width to, go to Format in the Cells group of the Home tab, and select AutoFit Column Width.

This is a long title, which we don't want to fit the column				
Books				
Stationery				
Frozen produce				
Recorded media				

serting
ultiple rows or columns

show you how to quickly insert multiple rows. You can
a similar technique to insert columns.

1 Click the number of the row where you want to
insert above, and drag down for as many rows as
you want to insert. For the example here, I want to
insert three rows above row 4.

A	B	C	D	E	F	G	H
		Jan	Feb	Mar	Apr	May	Jun
	Tractors	247	750	500	145	165	400
	Diggers	325	155	600	655	750	530
	Dump trucks	125	300	932	800	600	400

2 Click Insert in the Cells group of the Home tab. You
could alternatively use Ctrl with the plus symbol
(+). You can use the + key on your number
keypad or add Shift to the key combination to use
the key on the main keyboard.

A	B	C	D	E	F	G	H
		Jan	Feb	Mar	Apr	May	Jun
	Tractors	247	750	500	145	165	400
	Diggers	325	155	600	655	750	530
	Dump trucks	125	300	932	800	600	400

3 If you're inserting a row to copy another row into
it, you can save time by copying the row first.
When you insert, your copied row will be pasted
into the new row(s).

9

Managing
large spreadsheets

There are several techniques that can help you to manage large spreadsheets.

1 On the View tab, click New Window to see your worksheet in another window at the same time. You can scroll around in the windows independently, but it's just two views of the same document. Any changes you make will be visible both windows. Use Arrange All on the View tab organize your windows side by side.

2 Keep column and/ or row headings in view when you scroll. Also on the View tab, Freeze Panes can keep the top row or first column in view. You can

freeze both by selecting the cell that is underneat the column heading and to the right of the row heading that you want to keep, and then choosin Freeze Panes. Using this approach, you can freeze several rows or columns.

3 Focus on what's important by hiding rows and columns you don't need right now. Select the rows or columns (click and

drag on their letters or numbers in the margin), and choose Hide Rows or Hide Columns. These options are on the Home tab, in the Editing grou under the Format menu.

o improve data quality, you can validate data as it is
ntered into the spreadsheet.

1 Select the cells you want to apply validation to.

2 Click Data Validation on the Data tab of the
ribbon. The Data Validation options open.

3 In the Allow menu, you can choose to allow any
value (the default), whole numbers, decimals,
dates, times, or text of a certain length. You can
also define custom validation (see Tip 9) or use a
list of valid data items (see Tip 8).

4 In the Data menu, you can choose a sequence
of valid values (between), minimum and/or
maximum values, or a sequence of invalid values
(not between). Use the boxes below to enter the
start and end dates, or minimum and maximum
numbers. Use the Input Message tab to give users
instructions on entering valid data. Instructions are
shown when users select the cell.

Adding a drop-down menu

You can ensure data is valid and speed up its entry by putting a drop-down menu in a cell. This is one of the data validation options.

1 Select the cell(s) where you want to use the menu

2 Click Data Validation on the Data tab of the ribbon to open the Data Validation options. There's a shortcut: press ALT, D, and L one at a time.

3 In the Allow drop-down menu, choose List.

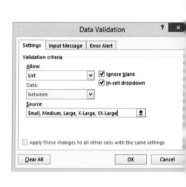

4 In the Source box, type the menu items, separated by a comma. Click OK.

5 If you prefer, you can use data that's in a spreadsheet row, column, or named range (see p.41). In that case, enter an = sign followed by the name in the Source box, or enter = there and then select the menu items on the spreadsheet using the mouse. It's easy to edit your menu later by simply editing those cells.

6 When you select one of the cells, a menu will appear so you can select the data you'd like to enter in that cell.

reating custom validation

u can write your own validation rules. Select the cell(s)
u want to validate and go to the Data Validation options
e Tip 7). Select Custom in the Allow menu. In the Formula
x, enter a formula that gives a result of TRUE or FALSE.
re are some examples to validate cell J8:

Must start with text "CPC". =COUNTIF(J8, "CPC*")=1

Length must be 3. =LEN(J8)=3

Must be a number. =ISNUMBER(J8)

First character must be a number. The LEFT function
is used to extract the character, and ISNUMBER is
used to test whether it is a number. The VALUE
function is required because in a data item like
"UK-52", the 52 would otherwise be treated as text.
=ISNUMBER(VALUE(LEFT(J8,1)))

Last character must not be a number. To see whether
a character is not a number, we can check whether it
is a number, and then wrap it in the NOT function to
reverse the result.
=NOT(ISNUMBER(VALUE(RIGHT(J8,1))))

Must be unique in column J. This shows an error if
the same data has already been entered in the same
column. =COUNTIF(J:J, J8)<=1

Must be odd. =ISODD(J8). ISEVEN can be used, too.

allow multiple options, join them with OR, like this
mple, which allows data of 3 or 5 characters to be valid:

R(LEN(J8)=3, LEN(J8)=5)

enforce multiple validation rules, use AND, like this
mple, which requires a 3-character code starting with A:

ND(LEN(J8)=3, COUNTIF(J8, "A*")=1)

13

You can remove duplicated data in a spreadsheet, which can easily happen if data such as mailing list information combined from multiple sources.

1 Click in your data so Excel can find it.

2 Click Remove Duplicates on the Data tab of the ribbon. You'll find it in the Data Tools group.

3 Select the columns that you want to check for duplicate entries. It's safest to keep them all selected. If you just selected the First Name and Last Name (for example), two different people w share a name would be identified as duplicates, even though they have different addresses. One them would be automatically deleted. This doesn happen if you select the address fields as well.

4 Click OK. Beware, though, as that might delete rows from your spreadsheet. Use Undo immediately to bring them back if you made a mistake.

u might be storing the same person twice, at their new
d their old address. You can highlight duplicated data so
u can fix it manually.

1 Select the cells you want to check for duplicates.
In a mailing list spreadsheet, this might be the First
Name and Last Name columns.

2 On the Home tab, click Conditional Formatting.
Select Highlight Cells Rules and choose Duplicate
Values.

3 You can choose to
highlight duplicate
or unique values,
and can pick your
preferred color and
formatting option.

4 This isn't smart enough to recognize first and
second name combinations, so all the occurrences
of Ben would be highlighted, even if they have
different surnames. Even if the first name and
surname are both highlighted, it might not be
a repeated person, because the names might be
shared with different people. It's a good first pass
for a manual review, though.

st Name	Last Name	Street	City	Postcode	Country
ger	Anout	99 Penny Lane	Liverpool	L2 0LL	UK
bin	Banks	99 Mansion Row	Birmingham	B4 9ET	UK
tin	Case	87 Grantchester Meadows	London	MSO 0AW	UK
	Case	87 Grantchester Meadows	London	MSO 0AW	UK
n	Debusse	45 Rhyming Drive	London	MSO 0AW	UK
	Dente	555 Americas Avenue	London	W4 4JJ	UK
n	Debusse	52 Politti Street	London	MSO 0AW	UK
n	Elux	12 Disney Matter Road	Glasgow	G1 1QQ	UK
ward	Eineau	88 Lucky Street	Bracknell	RG12 4LU	UK
adge	Ination	12 Disney Matter Road	Glasgow	G1 1QQ	UK

There are lots of advanced paste options. Cells can contain formulas, values (which are formula results, or numbers or text entered directly) and formatting. You can paste each of these independently.

Click the arrow on the Paste button on the Home tab to find advanced paste options. For example, you can paste:

● Formulas and number formatting (such as currencies) without overwriting other formatting.

● Values only. This is useful if you want to copy the result of a formula, but not the formula itself.

● Formatting only (see also Tip 67 – the Format Painter

● Everything except borders.

● Everything, keeping the original column widths.

● Everything, but transposing (or swapping over) the rows and columns. Here's an example: Compare the left table with the right one.

	Tractors	Diggers	Dump trucks
Jan	247	325	125
Feb	750	155	300
Mar	500	600	932

	Jan	Feb	Mar
Tractors	247	750	5
Diggers	325	155	6
Dump trucks	125	300	9

Paste Special includes the option to skip blanks or to carry out a mathematical operation. For example, copy 2 and paste with Divide to halve the numbers you paste over. To make negative numbers positive, copy -1 and paste it on of the negative numbers with the Multiply option.

xpanding the clipboard

you're moving lots of information
ound, you can use the clipboard to
re multiple items you've copied.

1 Click the tiny arrow to the right of the Clipboard label on the Home tab.

2 The clipboard expands into a column on the left. You can click any of the items in the clipboard to paste them at your cursor's current position.

3 Click the menu button that appears when you hover over an item in the clipboard, and you can choose to delete that item. This is useful if the clipboard contains data you no longer need and it's getting in the way.

4 You can empty the whole clipboard by clicking Clear All at the top.

5 You can use Paste All at the top of the clipboard to paste all the data in one go. You might get unexpected results if the data is not similar in its structure, because you've been copying from different parts of the spreadsheet.

There is an easier way to move data around your spreadsheet than copying and pasting it.

1 Select the data you want to move by clicking the start cell and dragging with the mouse.

2 Move your mouse cursor over one of the edges of the selected area. The cursor becomes a four-headed arrow.

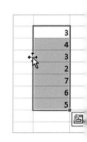

3 Click and drag with your mouse. An outline will follow your mouse cursor showing how much space the selected area will occupy.

4 Release the mouse button to drop the data in its new position on the spreadsheet.

You can use that technique to move an entire row or column after selecting it, but it will overwrite what's alread in the cells you move to. Alternatively, you can cut a colum and then insert a new column and paste your data into it a the same time. This also works for rows.

1 Select the column you want to move. You can select several consecutive columns to move using Shift + click to select the first and last one.

2 Use Ctrl + X to cut the data.

3 Select the column to the right of where you want to insert a new column. Click Insert on the Home tab of the ribbon to move the columns you cut.

re are some tips for entering formulas in cells.

1 If you don't know the name of the function you need, you can click the fx button beside the formula bar to search for it by description.

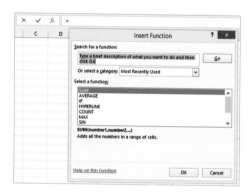

2 When you're entering a function name, Excel can help you complete it. A menu opens with function names that match what you've typed so far. You see a description of the function too. Use the Up and Down arrows to choose an option. Use Tab to select the option. You can then use Shift + Ctrl + A to have placeholder values inserted in your formula. For example:
=MAX(number1,number2,...)

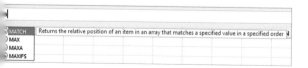

3 If you've named cells or ranges (see Tip 37), tap F3 to paste a name from a menu into your formula.

Understandin
formula symbol

Here's a handy reference to the symbols used in formulas:

- All formulas start with =

- Use $ to fix cell
  references. When I
  copied the formula
  from cell C2 into C3
  and C4, it updated the
  row references in the

	A	B	C
1	Cows	Sheep	Total
2	5	6	=A2+B2
3	4	2	=A3+B3
4	1	3	=A4+B4

  formula. As a result, cell C4 adds up the cows (A4) and
  sheep (B4) in that row, which is the expected result. If y
  don't want the row to change when you paste a formu
  put a $ in front of it (for example, A$2). If you don't
  want the column to change, put a $ in front of that
  (for example, $A2). You can fix both too (for example,
  A2). You do this in your formula before you copy i

- You can cycle through the options for fixing rows,
  columns, and both in a cell reference by tapping F4.

- Use a colon between cells to make a range. A2:A4 is
  the range of cells containing all the cows. A:A mean:
  all of column A, and 2:2 would be all of row 2.

- Put ! at the end of a sheet name. For example, to us
  cell C3 in Sheet6 from a different worksheet, your ce
  reference would be Sheet6!C3.

- Put parentheses () around the data used by function:
  Each opening parenthesis needs a closing one.

- Use + for addition.

- Use - for subtraction.

- Use * for multiplication.

- Use / for division.

inding the highest/ owest value in a range

u can use the MAX function to find the highest value
latest date) in a range or set of numbers. There is an
uivalent function called MIN that you can use to find the
west number (or the earliest date) from a range.

1 Click on the cell where you want the result to be.

2 Type in =MAX(

3 Select the cells with the mouse, or type in the
range coordinates.

4 If you want to add another range, type a comma
and then select the new range.

5 Press Enter to add the closing parenthesis) and see
the result in the spreadsheet.

u can access both MIN and MAX using the Autosum
tton on the Home tab:

1 Select the range you want to analyze, typically a
column or row of numbers.

2 Click the small
arrow beside the
Autosum button on
the Home tab.

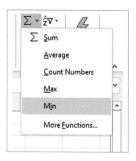

3 When the menu opens,
click Min or Max. The
result is added at the
end of your range.

21

Ranking data item

You can use the RANK function to show you how a data item ranks compared to others. For example, you can use i to quickly spot the biggest sale, without sorting the data.

The RANK function works like this:

=RANK(cell you want to rank, cell range you want to compare it against, ranking order)

The ranking order parameter at the end is optional. The default value of 0 is the order we usually use for bestsellin book and music charts, where 1 represents the biggest sel and the rank numbers increase for lower sales volumes.

Add a ranking order of 1 to reverse the order, so the lowes value is ranked 1. For example, you might use this when comparing speed, based on the time taken (the fastest car took the least time).

If you want to copy your RANK function down your colum remember to add a $ before the row numbers for the comparison range so they aren't changed as the function is copied. For example, looking at the worksheet below, m function to rank the first sales figure in column B is:

=RANK(B2,B$2:B$7)

I've copied this formula down column D.

	A	B	C	D
1	Date	Sales	RANK	REVERSE
2	May-25	10764	3	4
3	Jun-25	7338	6	1
4	Jul-25	7436	5	2
5	Aug-25	14162	1	6
6	Sep-25	9360	4	3
7	Oct-25	11529	2	5

nding an item by
s ranking using LARGE

MAX and MIN functions give you the highest and
west numbers in a range. To find an item at other
sitions in the ranking, use the LARGE function.

Click on the cell where you want the result to be.

Type in =LARGE(

Select the cells with the mouse, or type in the
range coordinates. In my screenshot, the range
is sorted so you can easily check the data. This
function is probably most helpful when the data
isn't already sorted.

Type a comma, followed by the position number of
the item you want to find. For example, to find the
second biggest number in the range, use 2.

When you've finished, press Enter to complete the
formula and see the result in the spreadsheet.

	A	B
1	Agent	Sales
2	Alex	15
3	Chris	27
4	Charlie	34
5	Frankie	48
6	Ashley	56
7	Jordan	68
8	Casey	72
9		
10	MAX(B2:B8)	72
11	LARGE(B2:B8, 2)	68
12	MIN(B2:B8)	15
13		

Excel provides three functions to find the average value from a range of cells.

If you wanted to find the average of the values in the cells A1 to A10, you could use:

- =AVERAGE(A1:A10). This is the average most people think of first: it's calculated by adding up all the values and then dividing by the number of data items. It's the arithmetic mean.

- =MEDIAN(A1:A10). This is the value in the middle of the range when it is sorted in number order. That's how it works if your list has an odd number of items. If your list has an even number of items, there is no item in the middle, so this gives the mid-point between the two middle items. In that case, it returns a number that is not in your range.

- =MODE(A1:A10). This returns the most frequently occurring value, irrespective of whether it is high or low, or somewhere in between.

You can use the Autosum menu on the Home tab of the ribbon to calculate the average (arithmetic mean).

If you just want to do a quick check of the average, highlight the cells and look at the status bar in the bottom right. If your monitor is wide enough, it shows the average, count, and sum for the selected range.

		5
		5
		30
		40
		50
		60
		5
		80
		30
		100
	Average	40.5
	Median	35
	Mode	5

u might find data is not in the right order. Let's sort it!

1 Click a cell in the column you wish to sort if you're sorting all your data, or select the data to sort.

2 On the Home tab, in the Editing group, click Sort & Filter. If available, select the option you require, such as sort Oldest to Newest, Newest to Oldest, Smallest to Largest, or Largest to Smallest.

3 It is possible to sort by multiple criteria – for example, sort first by date and then sort by the size of the sales within each month. If you need to sort by two or more criteria, click Custom Sort in the Sort & Filter menu.

4 Use the Add Level, Delete Level and Copy Level buttons to add or remove sorting criteria.

5 In the Sort On menu, you can sort by cell color, font color, and conditional formatting icon, as well as the cell value.

6 If you need to sort left to right instead of top to bottom, click Options and change the orientation.

Filters show you only the rows that contain certain values.

1 Click in the data where you want to add a filter.

2 On the Home ribbon, in the Editing group, open the Sort & Filter menu. Click Filter.

3 Filter buttons are added to your column headers. Click one to open the options. Select which values from that column you want view.

4 Click OK, and you see only the rows that contain your chosen values. Where a filter is active, there is an icon in the Filter button at the top of the column. The row numbers may also tell us that some rows are not shown. In my example below, I've filtered the product category to show only "Gardens" sales. You can filter seve columns at the same time, so I could use the filte in the Customer column to see sales of Garden equipment to ABC, for example. Use Clear Filter i the Filter options (shown in the picture above) to turn off the filter.

	A	B	C	D
1	Order Number ▼	Customer ▼	Product category ⊤	Sales Value
3	1266	Bigg Records	Gardens	1
5	1268	Roger's Plumbing	Gardens	7
7	1270	Syd's Home Construction	Gardens	1
9	1272	Nick's Masonry Services	Gardens	
11	1274	Rick's Stationery	Gardens	
12	1275	ABC	Gardens	

Excel can decide what should be in a cell using the IF function. It uses this format:

=IF(decision criterion, cell value if true, cell value if false)

For example, here's a spreadsheet showing monthly sales and sales targets.

	A	B	C	D
1	**Month**	**Sales by month**	**Target**	**On target?**
2	Apr-19	11555	10000	
3	May-19	10764	11000	Missed target
4	Jun-19	12194	9500	
5	Jul-19	7338	9500	Missed target

I used this formula in cell D2 then copied it down column D:

=IF(B2 >= C2, "", "Missed target")

The "" is an empty value, so column D is empty when the target has been achieved, and the warnings stand out.

You can use all the operators for your comparison:

= to test whether two values are the same.

<> to test whether two values are not the same.

> to check if the first value is more than the second.

< to check if the first value is less than the second.

>= to ask whether the first value is more than or equal to the second.

<= to ask whether the first value is less than or equal to the second.

Combining IF function

You can combine IF functions together, by putting one insid another. This is called nesting them. For example, let's say you wanted to label a number as high, medium, or low, depending on its value. A value of 100 or lower is low, 10 to 200 is medium, and over 200 is high.

You can check whether a value in cell F4 is low, like this:

=IF(F4 <= 100, "low", "not low")

You can check whether a value is high, like this:

=IF(F4 > 200, "high", "not high")

We want to combine these functions, so that Excel works through this thought process:

● Is the number less than or equal to 100? If so, it's lov

● If it isn't a low number, let's see whether the number higher than 200. If so, it's a high number.

● If it's not a high number, and we know it's not a low number, then it must be medium.

Instead of just displaying "not low" when the value isn't low, we can go straight into another IF function that chec whether it's high. This is what it looks like, all together:

=IF(F4 <= 100, "low", IF(F4 > 200, "high", "medium"))

Excel 2016 introduced the IFS function, which is easier to use. You give it a list of decision criteria and the cell value true. To create a default value for when none of the criteri is true, provide a final decision criterion of TRUE with a default value. Here's our high/medium/low cell labeler aga

=IFS(F4 <= 100, "low", F4 > 200, "high",
TRUE, "medium")

create a total, you can use the SUM function. You provide
with a range of cells you want to sum. Here's an example
readsheet showing money received.

	A	B	C
1	Category	Sale Value	Received
2	Cutlery	346	Jun-22
3	Crockery	480	Jun-22
4	Cookware	251	May-22
5	Crockery	432	Aug-22
6	Cookware	284	Jul-22
7	Cutlery	423	Jun-22
8	Cookware	439	Sep-22
9	Cleaning	410	May-22
10	Cutlery	510	Apr-22
11	Cleaning	402	Aug-22
12	Total	3977	

To create the total in cell B12, you can enter
=SUM(B2:B11) into cell B12. You can type in the cell
range, or you can select the range using the mouse
after you type the opening parenthesis in the formula.

You can also use the Autosum button on the Home
tab of the ribbon. Put your cursor in cell B12 then click
the Autosum button. It will enter the SUM formula and
automatically select the range.

Even quicker: use the keyboard shortcut. Click on cell
B12 and then press Alt + = to enter the SUM formula
and automatically select the range.

You can also use this shortcut and the Autosum button
to total cells to the left in the current row.

Choosing value
to sum with SUMI

Sometimes, you might want to total up some of your data but not all of it. For example, you might want to get the sales receipts from June 2022 only.

You can use the SUMIF function to do this. The format is:

=SUMIF(range to compare, value to compare that rang against, data range to add up)

Here's a breakdown of those three parts to the formula:

● The cells you want to compare against.

● The value you want to compare them to – for examp "Jun-22". The value you want to compare will usually be in quotation marks – for example, "Jun-22" for a date, ">21" for values of more than 21, or "blue" to match that word. You can match the contents of another cell by using its cell reference, but shouldn't use quotation marks with it (for example, D2). You don't need quotation marks around a number, either.

● The cells you want to total.

To add up all the sales in June 2022 in rows 2 to 10 of th spreadsheet shown below you would enter this into a cell:
=SUMIF(C2:C10, "Jun-22", B2:B10)

Beware: If the range you're adding up is smaller than the range you're comparing in any direction, the range you're adding may be extended, leading to unexpected results.

	A	B	C
1	Category	Sale Value	Received
2	Cutlery	346	Jun-22
3	Crockery	480	Jun-22
4	Cookware	251	May-22
5	Crockery	432	Aug-22
6	Cookware	284	Jul-22

sing several
um criteria with SUMIFS

metimes, you might want to select data for totaling
ng more than one criterion. For example, using our sales
readsheet again (see Tip 26), you might want to total the
es receipts in June 2022 for cutlery. That involves checking
e values of two different cells (category and date), before
:aling up the number in a third cell (sale value).

do that, you use the SUMIFS function.

e catch is that the data to sum and the criteria are
tered in a different order when you use SUMIFS,
mpared to SUMIF. You enter data in this order:

The data you want to total.

The first range of cells you want to evaluate.

The value you want to compare them to.

The second range of cells you want to evaluate.

The value you want to compare them to.

e format is:

**UMIFS(data to add up, range to compare, value to
npare that range against, second range to compare,
ue to compare that range against)**

I can use more criteria if you wish: you don't have to
p at two.

add up the cutlery sales from June 2022 in our example
eadsheet (see Tip 26), we'd use:

UMIFS(B2:B10, C2:C10, "Jun-22", A0:A10, "Cutlery")

e size and shape of the ranges you are adding up and the
ges containing your criteria must be the same.

A cumulative sum is the "total so far". For example, if you'
working on a calendar year, March's total would include th
data for March, February, and January, to show the sales ir
the year up to that point. Cumulative sums can be useful
benchmarking performance against previous years.

There isn't a built-in function to calculate cumulative sums
but you can use the SUM function to do this. The solution
to fix the starting cell for the range you want to sum, but
leave the end cell as a relative reference.

	A	B	C
1	**Month**	**Sales**	**Cumulative total**
2	Jan	500	500
3	Feb	400	900
4	Mar	600	1500
5	Apr	400	1900
6	May	200	2100
7	Jun	100	2200

Here's a worked example:

1 We want to calculate the cumulative total of the
sales that are shown in column B. In cell C2, ent
=SUM(B$2:B2). (The start and end of the range
are the same here, because there's only one mor
to total.)

2 Copy the formula down the column.

3 As the formula is copied, the end of the range
will be updated. For example, in June, the formu
becomes =SUM(B$2:B7). Fixing the first cell
reference in the formula means it always starts
totaling with January's sales figures.

4 You can ignore the warnings that adjacent cells
not included in the formula.

Using SUMPRODUCT

Working out a grand total sometimes involves multiplying different values together. For example, your spreadsheet might show the price and quantity sold for each item.

You could calculate the sales value for each item by multiplying the quantity sold by the price, and then adding all these values up. But the SUMPRODUCT function does this in a single step for you.

The function works like this:

=SUMPRODUCT(first range, second range)

It is possible to add additional ranges to multiply together. You could, for example, add a third column with the percentage margin for each item to work out the profit on the goods sold.

	A	B	C
1	**Item**	**Price**	**Quantity sold**
2	Standard ice cream	2.5	300
3	Double scoop	3.5	200
4	Deluxe	5	100

Here's a worked example.

1 Put the unit price in column B.

2 Put the quantity sold in column C.

3 The grand total will be the sum of the unit price multiplied by the quantity for each row. To work this out, use =SUMPRODUCT(B2:B4, C2:C4)

Counting cell

There are four functions you can use to count cells. Let's imagine you want to count the cells in the range C1:C10. You could put one of these functions into another cell to se the result of the count. See the example below, where each function is used to count the column of data above:

- **=COUNT(C1:C10)**. This counts the number of cells containing numbers and dates, in the range given in parentheses. This can be useful if you don't want to count cells containing text, such as headings.

- **=COUNTA(C1:C10)**. This counts text, as well as numbers and dates. It gives you a total for the non-blank cells in your range.

- **=COUNTBLANK(C1:C10)**. This counts how many emp cells there are in the given range. You can use this to identify where your data might be incomplete.

- **=COUNTIF(C1:C10, ">25")**. The COUNTIF function enables you to count the number of cells that meet certain criteria. It's similar to SUMIF (see Tip 26). Insid the parentheses, you put the range first and then the criteria to match.

	10	a	a	a
	20	b	b	
	30	c	c	c
	40	d	d	
	50	e	e	e
	60	f	10	10
	70	g	20	
	80	h	30	30
	90	i	40	
	100	j	50	50
COUNT	10	0	5	3
COUNTA	10	10	10	6
COUNTBLANK	0	0	0	4
COUNTIF(range, ">25")	8	0	3	2

You can count cells that meet several criteria using the COUNTIFS function. It takes this form:

COUNTIFS(range to compare, value to compare against, second range to compare, second value to compare against...)

In the spreadsheet below, we want to count the number of orders delivered to London worth more than $400.

1 Click on the cell where you want the result to be.

2 Enter =COUNTIFS(

3 Click at the top of column K to select the column.

4 Type a comma, and then "London".

5 Type a comma, and then select column N.

6 Type a comma, and then ">400". Press Enter.

7 Your final formula looks like this: =COUNTIFS(K:K, "London", N:N, ">400")

H	I	J	K	L	M	N
First Name	Last Name	Street	City	Postcode	Country	Order value
Roger	Anout	99 Penny Lane	Liverpool	L2 0LL	UK	500
Robin	Banks	99 Mansion Row	Birmingham	B4 9ET	UK	600
Justin	Case	87 Grantchester Meadows	London	MSO 0AW	UK	300
Ed	Case	87 Grantchester Meadows	London	MSO 0AW	UK	200
Ben	Debusse	45 Rhyming Drive	London	MSO 0AW	UK	800
Al	Dente	555 Americas Avenue	London	W4 4JJ	UK	900
Ida	Down	99 Redford Avenue	Bedford	BD15 8TT	UK	44
Ben	Elux	12 Disney Matter Road	Glasgow	G1 1QQ	UK	555
Howard	Eineau	88 Lucky Street	Bracknell	RG12 4LU	UK	850
Madge	Ination	12 Disney Matter Road	Glasgow	G1 1QQ	UK	921
Andy	Mann	44 Runtime Drive	London	MSO 0AW	UK	1000
Madge	Case	121 Tooth Street	London	RG12 4LU	UK	250

You can use wildcards to do an inexact match with a piece of text. A wildcard is a character that stands in for one or more other characters. Wildcards can be used with COUNTIF/COUNTIFS and SUMIF/SUMIFS as well as some other functions, but cannot be used with IF.

There are three wildcards:

● **? (question mark)**. Stands in for any single character. For example, "a?e" would match both "ape" and "ace" but not "apple".

● *** (asterisk)**. Matches any number of characters. For example, "cut*" would match both "cutlery" and "cutlass".

● **~ (tilde)**. Is used before a * or ? if you actually want look for one in the text.

Here are some examples, based on counting the cells in the range A1 to A10:

● **=COUNTIF(A1:A10, "<>??-????")**. Checks for cells that do not contain data in the form of two character a dash, and then four characters. Checks like this can be used for validating order numbers and similar code Note that blank cells are counted in this case, so don' set the range as the whole column.

● **=COUNTIF(A1:A10, "BB*")**. Counts orders beginning with the letters BB.

● **=COUNTIF(A1:A10, "*~?")**. Counts cells that end wi a question mark. The * stands in for any number of characters at the start of the text. The tilde is required so Excel knows you want to match a question mark, not use it as a wildcard.

make it easier to understand your spreadsheet, you can
oup rows or columns. You can easily hide and show
oups using buttons in the margin.

1 If your data includes summary rows (see
screenshot), Excel can automatically create groups.
Click in your data. In the Outline group of the Data
tab, open the Group menu and select Auto Outline.

	A	B	C	D
1	Date	Region A	Region B	Region C
2	Jun-22	500	165	700
3	Jun-22	600	223	700
4	Jun-22	740	437	600
5	JUN total	1840	825	2000
6	Jul-22	400	100	600
7	Jul-22	500	200	500
8	Jul-22	600	100	400
9	JUL total	1500	400	1500
10	Aug-22	440	500	200
11	Aug-22	440	560	230
12	Aug-22	440	570	240
13	AUG total	1320	1630	670
14				

2 Alternatively, select the rows or columns you
want to combine into a group. They must be
consecutive: you can't have an unselected row or
column in the middle.

3 In the Outline group of the Data tab, click Group.
This combines your selected data into a group.

4 Use the + and - signs in the left and top margins
to show and hide your groups.

5 You can create a group inside another group.

6 To clear a group, select the rows/columns in the
group and then click Ungroup. You can remove
all groups using the Clear Outline option under
Ungroup. It doesn't delete any data.

Excel's subtotal feature does the work of the SUM function combined with automatic grouping.

1 Sort your data so it's organized how you want to subtotal it. For example, if you want to subtotal your expenses monthly, sort your data by month.

2 Click in your data.

3 On the Data tab of the ribbon, in the Outline group, click Subtotal.

4 In the first menu option, tell Excel how you want to group your data. For example, you might want to generate a subtotal for each month change.

5 Choose the function you want to use. Typically, this will be Sum. But you can also count items, calculate an average, and show the maximum or minimum values, among other things.

6 Select which columns you want to be subtotaled and click OK.

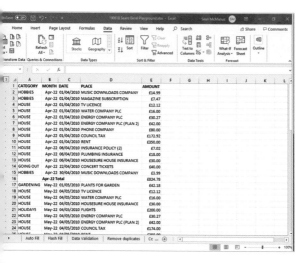

is is how you can use automatically generated subtotals.

1 Click the minus sign beside a subtotal to close the group, leaving only the subtotal visible.

2 Click the 1 button above the left margin to see the grand total of all the subtotaled items.

3 Click the 2 button above the left margin to see the subtotals. You can expand any of them by clicking the plus button beside it.

4 Click the 3 button above the left margin to see all your data again.

5 To remove your subtotal, click Subtotal on the ribbon. It's in the Outline group of the Data tab. In the options that appear, click Remove All.

When you copy data, any cells that are hidden will be copied with it. For example, any groups you've closed or rows you've hidden will be copied.

1 Select the data you want to copy, which may include hidden groups.

2 On the Home tab, in the Editing group, open the Find & Select menu. Click Go To Special... (see image on the right). The shortcut is Ctrl + G.

3 In the Go To Special menu, shown below, select "Visible cells only".

4 Click OK.

5 Now you can copy and paste in the usual way, using Ctrl + C to copy, and Ctrl + V to paste.

Naming ranges

You can simplify your formulas by naming ranges. For example, if you name a range "sales", you could use the formulas =SUM(sales) or =AVERAGE(sales). Names cannot include spaces, but you can use an underscore character.

1 Select the range you want to name.

2 The Name box is beside the formula bar. It usually contains the selected cell reference, or the size of the selected range while you are selecting it. Type in the name you want to use and press the Enter key.

3 Alternatively, you can click Define Name on the Formulas tab of the ribbon. Here, you can add a comment, and change the scope if you want the name to only apply to this worksheet and not the whole workbook. You can edit the range the name refers to in the "Refers to" box.

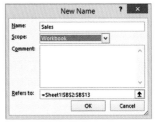

4 You can also put a number or a formula in the "Refers to" box. For example, you could define a name as =20% for discount calculations. If you change this value later, formulas based on the name recalculate. You could give a name to a formula =SUM(C:C) to avoid re-entering it each time you want to use the sales total.

You can see the name of a range in the Name box if you select the whole range. The most useful way to see and manage your named ranges and values, though, is to use the Name Manager.

1 On the Formulas tab of the ribbon, click Name Manager to open it.

2 Click a name to see the range, constant number, or formula it refers to at the bottom of the Name Manager pane.

3 Double-click a name or select it and click Edit if you want to change what it refers to. You can't change a name's scope once it's been defined.

4 Select a name and click Delete to delete it.

5 Use the filter in the top right to show names with errors. Excel will adjust the named range if you ac or remove data within the range, but if you delete all of the data in the named range, it causes an error. Any cells using the name will show #REF.

u can use the VLOOKUP function to find a value in a set of
ta, and use it in a formula. The function works by searching
column for your data. (If you haven't used VLOOKUP before,
Index-Match instead – see Tips 41 & 42).

OOKUP works like this:

**VLOOKUP(data to match, range to find it in, column
mber in that range where your desired data is, type of
atch)**

easiest to understand with a worked example.

	A	B	C	
1	**Item**	**Price**	**Quantity sold**	
2	Standard ice cream	2.5	300	
3	Double scoop	3.5	200	
4	Deluxe ice cream	5	100	
5	Lollies	1.25	200	
6	Crisps	1	120	
7	Canned drink	1	400	
8				

this spreadsheet, let's say we want to look up the
antity of crisps sold. (We'll use the text "Crisps" but you
uld use a cell reference to search for a cell's contents
tead.) The data is in the range A1:C7. The word we're
king for must always be in the first column of the range,
d we call that column number 1. The quantity sold is in
umn 3, then. There are two types of match you can use.
an exact match, use FALSE.

s is what the final formula would look like:

VLOOKUP("Crisps", A1:C7, 3, FALSE)

e other match type is an inexact match (chosen using
JE), where the function returns the nearest value lower
n the chosen value. You might want to use this when
J're looking up numbers instead of text.

The HLOOKUP function is similar to VLOOKUP (see Tip 39). Yc use it to find a value in a set of data, but you search acros a row to find the data. If this is the first time you've come across HLOOKUP, try Index-Match instead (see Tips 41 & 42

HLOOKUP works like this:

=HLOOKUP(data to match, range to find it in, row number in that range where your desired data is, type c match)

	A	B	C	D
1	Date	Spanners	Hammers	Drills
2	June	100	200	300
3	July	400	500	600
4	August	700	800	900
5				
6	Spanners	100		

In the spreadsheet shown here, let's say we want to be ab to look up the June sales for different product categories. We want to be able to type the product we're interested in into cell A6, and then see the sales volume for that item in cell B6. Obviously, we can see that at a glance in this simple example, but the same idea applies to much bigger worksheets, and to looking up across different worksheets.

The text we're searching for is in cell A6 and the data is in the range B1:D4. The first row must contain the data we'r searching for. The first row is number 1, so our data (for June) is in row 2. We use the match type of FALSE to ensu there is an exact match. A match type of TRUE would retu the nearest lower value if there isn't an exact match.

Here's what our formula would look like:

=HLOOKUP(A6, B1:D4, 2, FALSE)

e VLOOKUP and HLOOKUP functions are fairly limited: you
n only look up values to the right (VLOOKUP) or below
.OOKUP) the data you search for, and you need to know
e number of rows/columns away your desired data is. If
u insert rows/columns, you can break the formula. That's
y it's better to use a combination of the INDEX and
ATCH functions.

e MATCH function is used to find the position of an item
thin a range of cells. It works like this:

**MATCH(data to match, range to find it in – must be a
ngle row or column, type of match)**

e type of match is optional. Use 0 to force an exact
tch. The default option (1) returns the largest value up
and including your data to match. Use -1 to find the
allest value equal to, or above, your data.

example, let's search for a food item in the spreadsheet
ow. We'll put the item we want to find in cell A9. Our
od items are in the range A2:A7. Here's the formula:

MATCH(A9, A2:A7, 0)

e returned value is 4, because "Lollies" is the
rth item in the range.

	A	B	C
1	Item	Price	Quantity sold
2	Standard ice cream	2.5	300
3	Double scoop	3.5	200
4	Deluxe ice cream	5	100
5	Lollies	1.25	200
6	Crisps	1	120
7	Canned drink	1	400
8			
9	Lollies	4	
10			

The INDEX function returns a particular data item, given its position in a range. The range must be in a single column row. The function is structured like this:

=INDEX(range, item number)

For example, using our ice cream shop example (see Tip 41), we can look up the second item in the sales list (range A2:A7) using:

=INDEX(A2:A7,2)

This returns the value "Double scoop" as you would expec

The INDEX function is most powerful when combined with the MATCH function. You can replace the item number in the range with a MATCH function, which can generate an item number by searching in another range. Then, INDEX can be a flexible replacement for VLOOKUP and HLOOKUP.

For example, to find the quantity of lollies sold, we'd use:

=INDEX(C2:C7, MATCH("Lollies", A2:A7, 0))

Here's a ready reference for that combination:

=INDEX(range containing data to return, MATCH(data search for, range to find it in, type of match))

You can use INDEX together with both a row number and column number. The range doesn't need to be a single ro column when you do that:

=INDEX(A2:C7, row number, column number)

MATCH can replace both the row and column numbers. Here's an example, which searches the rows for "Lollies" a the columns for "Price" and returns the number in that ce

=INDEX(A3:C8, MATCH("Lollies",A2:A7,0),
MATCH("Price",A1:C1,0))

e CHOOSE function is used to select an item from a list
items provided in the function. You provide the position
mber of the item you want, followed by a list of the
ms. The items can be numbers, pieces of text, or ranges.

s is how you use the CHOOSE function:

:HOOSE(item number you want, list of items separated
  commas)

· example:

:HOOSE(4, "Monday", "Tuesday", "Wednesday",
ıursday", "Friday", "Saturday", "Sunday")

s would give you "Thursday".

ı can use a cell reference in place of the item number:

:HOOSE(A6, "Monday", "Tuesday", "Wednesday",
ıursday", "Friday", "Saturday", "Sunday")

ou type 3 into cell A6, you'll see "Wednesday" in the
 containing this CHOOSE function. If you don't provide a
d item number, you'll see an error message in the cell.

ı can use CHOOSE to return a range, which can then be
d in other functions. For example:

UM(CHOOSE(2, B2:B7, C2:C7, D2:D7))

re, the CHOOSE function gives the range C2:C7 to the
M function to add up.

ou want to select a random item, use the RANDBETWEEN
ction. It takes the lowest and highest numbers for your
dom number. Random numbers change whenever the
eadsheet is recalculated. Try this:

HOOSE(RANDBETWEEN(1,7), "Monday", "Tuesday",
ednesday", "Thursday", "Friday", "Saturday", "Sunday")

You can use the buttons in the Number group of the Home tab to increase or decrease the number of decimal places a cell shows. This doesn't change the number, though, which can lead to odd results when you do sums with them. If you enter 0.25 in two cells and format to one decimal place, they'll be shown as 0.3. But they'll still add up to 0.5.

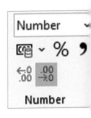

To fix this anomaly, round the numbers themselves using t ROUND function. It works like this:

=ROUND(cell reference, number of decimal digits)

1 Insert a new column (if necessary) beside your da

2 In a cell beside one of the figures you need to round, type in =ROUND(

3 Select the cell containing the data to round.

4 Enter a comma, followed by the number of decimal spaces you want to round to. For currencies, for example, enter 2.

5 Press Enter to add a closing parenthesis.

6 Your formula cell now contains the rounded value. Decimal digits of 5 or above are rounded up, and others are rounded down. You can copy the formula down to round other values in the column. Then, you can copy the cells with rounded numbers and paste their values over the unrounded data (see Tip 12).

The ROUND function is great for most purposes, but there are additional functions that give you more control over how data is rounded:

- **ROUNDUP(cell reference, number of decimal digits)**. This function always rounds numbers up. For example, ROUNDUP(2.111, 2) gives 2.12 and not 2.11. If you're rounding negative numbers, it rounds them away from zero.

- **ROUNDDOWN(cell reference, number of decimal digits)**. This function always rounds numbers down. For example, ROUNDDOWN(2.199, 2) gives 2.19 and not 2.2. If you're rounding negative numbers, it rounds them towards zero.

Raw data	ROUND	ROUNDUP	ROUNDDOWN
2.22	2.2	2.3	2.2
2.25	2.3	2.3	2.2
2.27	2.3	2.3	2.2
-2.22	-2.2	-2.3	-2.2
-2.25	-2.3	-2.3	-2.2
-2.27	-2.3	-2.3	-2.2

TRUNC(cell reference, number of decimal digits to keep). This function truncates (or shortens) the number by chopping off the decimal part. If you don't tell it how many digits to leave, it removes all of the decimal portion. TRUNC(2.777, 1) gives you 2.7. TRUNC(2.777) gives you the whole number 2.

MROUND(cell reference, multiple). This function is used to round to the nearest multiple of a number. For example, you could see which multiple of 10 is closest to a particular number. 22 would round to 20. 25 would round to 30.

You might have noticed that dates turn into (usually quite big) numbers if you format a date as a number.

That's because Excel doesn't store the date, month, and year of a date. Instead it records a date as the day number, counting from 1st January 1900. When Excel displays the date to you, it decodes it into the form you want to use.

Because dates are stored as numbers, you can perform simple calculations on them:

● You can work out how many days there are between two dates by just subtracting the earlier date from the later date, as this example shows:

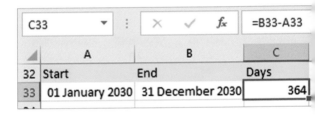

C33		✕	✓	f_x	=B33-A33
	A		B		C
32	Start		End		Days
33	01 January 2030		31 December 2030		364

There is also a function for this. **DAYS(end date, star date)** will count the days between two dates.

● You can add a number of days to a date. For example if your invoice is due in 30 days, you can work out th due date by adding the number 30 to the date the invoice was issued.

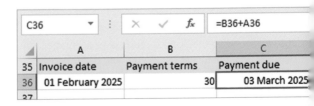

C36		✕	✓	f_x	=B36+A36
	A		B		C
35	Invoice date		Payment terms		Payment due
36	01 February 2025		30		03 March 2025

Making dates and breaking them down

Excel provides several functions for date handling. They make it easy to split the date up into its constituent parts, and help you compile your own dates in the correct format:

DAY(cell containing date). Extracts the day number from the date in the cell you give it.

MONTH(cell containing date). Pulls out the month number from the date.

YEAR(cell containing date). Extracts the year from the date in the cell.

	A	B	C
	Date	Formula	Result
9			
0	14 February 2025	=DAY(A40)	14
1	14 February 2025	=MONTH(A41)	2
2	14 February 2025	=YEAR(A42)	2025
3			

DATE(year, month, date). Creates a date in the correct Excel format, using the numbers you give it. Note that Excel cannot handle years before 1900. If you enter a lower number than 1900, it'll be added to 1900 to make a year later than 1900.

| 47 | ▾ | ⋮ | ✕ ✓ | *fx* | =DATE(A47,B47,C47) |

	A	B	C	D
	Year	Month	Day	Date
	2025	10	17	17 October 2025

48 Creating custom date format

You can create your own date formats. Click
the cell(s) containing the dates you want to
format, then click to expand the Number
group of the Home ribbon. Use the small
arrow beside where it says Number. To
create your own date format, click Custom
in the category list. In the Type box, enter the code for you
custom format. The code is made up of these symbols:

- **d**. Days as numbers 1 to 31.

- **dd**. Days as numbers 01 to 31.

- **ddd**. Short day names: Sun, Mon, Tue, etc.

- **dddd**. Full day names: Sunday, Monday, Tuesday, etc.

- **m**. Months as numbers 1 to 12.

- **mm**. Months as numbers 01 to 12.

- **mmm**. Short month names: Jan, Feb, Mar, etc.

- **mmmm**. Full month names: January, February, etc.

- **mmmmm**. The first letter of the month: J, F, M, etc.

- **yy**. Year as two digits – e.g. 25 for 2025.

- **yyyy**. Full four-digit year.

For example, to get a date in the form of **Friday, 31 Oct 2**
you would use: **dddd, dd mmm yy**.

Sample
Friday, 31 Oct 25
Type:
dddd, dd mmm yy

Within the ribbon image: General | % | .00 .00 | Number

Using multiple lines of text in cells

Here are some tips for working with lengthy text that spans multiple lines within the cell.

1 By default, text will spill out of the right of the cell and into other cells to the right of it. If data is entered into one of those other cells, it will cover your text, as shown here.

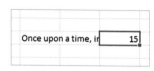

To fix this, click the cell with the text in and then click the Wrap Text button on the ribbon. It's in the Alignment group of the Home tab. (You can adjust the column width too – see Tip 4.)

2 To enter a line break when you're typing text into a cell, use Alt + Enter.

3 To edit your text more easily, expand the formula bar. Click it and drag the bottom of it down.

There are several functions you can use to clean your data to avoid unexpected outcomes later on, and to ensure your spreadsheet output looks right:

● **TRIM(cell containing text).** This function strips out all spaces at the start and end of text, and any extra spaces in the middle. Here's an example of the output below, with the length shown so you can see where there are spaces at the end.

C17	▼	:	×	✓	*fx*	=TRIM(A17)	

	A	B	C	D
15	Text	Length (untrimmed)	Trimmed text	Length (trimmed)
16	ABC	5	ABC	3
17	AB C	10	AB C	4
18	ABC	8	ABC	3

● **CLEAN(cell containing text).** This function strips out the first 32 non-printing characters in the character se including line breaks. You're only likely to need this if you've imported text from another computer system. I you see strange symbols in your data, this might help.

● **PROPER(cell containing text).** This function is used to capitalize the first letter of each word. It can clean up the formatting of names. It doesn't accurately capitali. names with a capital mid-way through, though (such as McCartney).

● **UPPER(cell containing text).** This converts the text to capital letters. You could use it to standardize order codes, for example.

● **LOWER(cell containing text).** This function converts text to lower case.

here are three ways you can join pieces of text:

- **The & operator**. Here's an example, where I've made an email address by joining the first name, a dot, last name, and the "@example.com" part of the address. Some of the text is in the spreadsheet cells, and some of it is in the formula. When you put text in a formula, you put quotation marks around it, "like this".

C2	▼	:	✕	✓	*fx*	=A2 & "." & B2 & "@example.com"

	A	B	C
	First name	Last name	Email address
	Willy	Orwonti	Willy.Orwonti@example.com

- **CONCAT(text to join, text to join...)**. This is short for concatenate, which basically means to join things up. Before Excel 2016, this was called CONCATENATE.

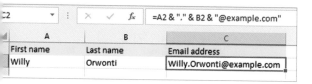

2	▼	:	✕	✓	*fx*	=CONCATENATE(A2, ".",B2, "@example.com")

	A	B	C	D
	First name	Last name	Email address	
	Al	Dente	Al.Dente@example.com	

- **TEXTJOIN(text to add between joined text, ignore empty?, text to join, text to join...)**. This function was new in Excel 2016. It's great for joining names because you can tell it to add a space between joined words, and to ignore empty cells. It works with a range too.

	▼	:	✕	✓	*fx*	=TEXTJOIN(" ",TRUE,A3:D3)

A	B	C	D	E
Title	First name	Middle name	Last name	Email address
Mr	Billy		Fish	Mr Billy Fish
	Sally	Jane	Smith	Sally Jane Smith
Dr	Alex	Chris	Jones	Dr Alex Chris Jones

In Excel (and many other computing arenas), a piece of text is called a string. It can be helpful to know the length of a string. For example, you might use a spreadsheet to organize social media content, and need to keep a close ey on character counts.

Tweets	Length
Download a free chapter from #Scratch Programming in Easy Steps here. [Link]	76

You can use the LEN function to count how many characte (including spaces) are in a piece of text.

1 Enter the text you want to know the length of.

2 In another cell where you would like to see the te length displayed, enter =LEN(

3 Click the cell containing the content you want the length of.

4 Type a closing parenthesis). Now, if you wanted to see the length of the text in cell A1, your cell would contain =LEN(A1)

5 Press Enter to see the length shown in your spreadsheet. The count includes any spaces in the string, even if they're at the end of the text in the cell you're counting. When the text in the cell changes, your text length will update automatica

ere are two Excel functions you can use to search inside
e text in a cell:

- The **FIND** function is case-sensitive, which means it
  treats capital and lower case letters as if they were
  different letters. If you look for a "k" in "Karen", you
  won't find it using FIND because the K in that string is
  capitalized. If you want an exact match, FIND is ideal.

- The **SEARCH** function is not case-sensitive, and it also
  enables you to use wildcards to search (see Tip 32).
  This is a more flexible option, and is the one you'll
  want to use most of the time. The exception might
  be if you want to search your text for an asterisk or a
  question mark. SEARCH will treat them as wildcards
  instead of looking for them in the text, unless you use
  a tilde before the asterisk or question mark. It might be
  simpler to use FIND instead in that case.

e result is the first position number where your text was
und in the cell you're searching. The count starts at 1 for
e first character in that cell. If the text you're looking for
not found in the text you're searching, you'll get the error
essage #VALUE.

th functions use a similar format:

FIND(text to find, cell to search, starting position)

SEARCH(text to find, cell to search, starting position)

e the optional starting position if you don't want to start
oking from the beginning of the text you're searching. For
ample:

SEARCH("hello", A1, 5)

arches cell A1 from the fifth character in that cell, for the
xt "hello" in any combination of upper or lower case.

Extracting pieces of text

There are three functions you can use to extract pieces of text or parts of a number from a cell:

- **LEFT(cell containing text, number of letters)**. Extract the first letters from a cell. If you don't include the number of letters, the function gives you the first lette

- **RIGHT(cell containing text, number of letters)**. Extracts the final letters from a cell. If you don't specif how many letters, the function gives you the last one.

- **MID(cell containing text, start position, number of letters)**. Extracts some text from the middle of the cel

For example, if cell A3 contains an order code and the first four letters indicate the product type, you could extract the product type using:

=LEFT(A3, 4)

Imagine you had a six-digit part number (e.g. 198542) in cell A23, where the middle two digits indicated the bin where they're stored in the warehouse (see screenshot below). You could extract the bin number using:

=MID(A23,3,2)

This gives us two digits, starting with the third digit (85). Note that you can use MID with numbers, as well as text.

B23	▼	:	× ✓	ƒx	=MID(A23,3,2)

◢	A	B	C
21	Part number	Warehouse bin	
22	375431	54	
23	198542	85	
24	154231	42	
25			

Splitting
first and last names

You might have a spreadsheet where each person's first and last name is combined in a single cell. You can use a combination of the LEFT, RIGHT, and FIND functions to split the names into separate cells. (See also Tip 3 & Tip 56.)

You use the FIND function to find the position of the space in the cell. You can then use that with the LEFT and RIGHT functions to pull out the first and last names.

To find the position of the space in cell A2, you would use:

FIND(" ", A2)

If the name is, for example, "George Harrison", the space is in position 7. We only need the first six characters for the name, so when we put the FIND function in place of the number of letters we want to extract, we subtract 1:

LEFT(A2, FIND(" ", A2) - 1)

B2	:	×	✓	fx	=LEFT(A2, FIND(" ",A2) - 1)	

	A	B	C
1	Full name	First name	Last Name
2	George Harrison	George	Harrison
3	John Lennon	John	Lennon
4	Paul McCartney	Paul	McCartney
5	Richard Starkey	Richard	Starkey

To work out how many letters to take from the right, we work out how long the whole name is and then subtract the position number of the space:

RIGHT(A2, LEN(A2) - FIND(" ", A2))

	A	B	C
	Full name	First name	Last Name
	George Harrison	George	Harrison
	John Lennon	John	Lennon

You can also split text (including first and last names) using the Text to Columns feature. This won't update the names when the joined name changes, unlike a formula (see Tip 55)

1 Select the cells containing the text to split.

2 Click the Data tab, and choose Text to Columns.

3 Choose "Delimited" if you want to separate text using spaces, commas, or other symbols. Choose "Fixed width" if you want to always have the same number of characters in each column. Click Next.

4 When you choose "Delimited", you can choose which symbols (or "delimiters") are used to split the column. If you're splitting

names, choose Space as your delimiter. Click Next.

5 Using "Fixed width", you click and drag lines to show where to split the text. Click Next.

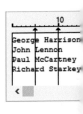

6 You can (optionally) choose the data format to use for each column by clicking the column in the data preview, then choosing the data format above. Click Finish.

replacing text in a cell

ere are two functions you can use to replace text:

SUBSTITUTE(cell containing text, characters you want
to replace, new characters you want to use, which
occurrence you want to replace). This will replace
the characters you specify with new characters. If you
miss out the last option, all of the occurrences will be
replaced. This function is useful if you want to change
words or phrases and you don't know (or don't mind)
where they are in the cell. Here's an example, where
the function is used to replace the word "November"
with "December" each time it occurs in the text:

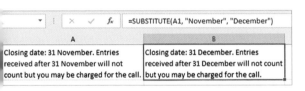

REPLACE(cell containing text, position number of
first character you want to replace, number of
characters you want to replace, new text). Use
REPLACE to change specific characters in the cell.
It might be useful if you have data such as order
codes, which follow a particular pattern. The number
of characters you replace and the number of new
characters you introduce can be different. You can
replace three characters with one character, for
example. Here, I replace three characters (BCD) starting
at position 2 (B), with the single character "X":

There isn't a built-in function to count the number of wor
in a cell, so it requires a formula. The formula works by
removing the spaces, and then seeing how much shorter t
resulting text is. You'll need the SUBSTITUTE (see Tip 57),
LEN (see Tip 52) and TRIM (see Tip 50) functions.

1 Start by getting the length of the text where you
want to count words. I'm using cell A1. To avoid
errors, we'll use TRIM to remove any extra spaces
Enter the following in the formula bar:
=LEN(TRIM(A1))

2 We're going to remove the spaces in the cell. We
use SUBSTITUTE to tell Excel to replace spaces wi
nothing, by using quotation marks with nothing
between them for the replacement text. (The firs
quotation marks contain a space.) We then need
wrap all of that in a LEN function to work out hc
long the string is now, and we're going to subtra
that from the length of the original string. Add t
new parts of your formula shown here:
=LEN(TRIM(A1)) - **LEN(SUBSTITUTE(A1," ",""))**

3 Finally, we need to add 1 to make it accurate,
because the last word doesn't have a space after
Your final formula is:
=LEN(TRIM(A1)) - LEN(SUBSTITUTE(A1," ","")) +

B1	▼	:	×	✓	ƒx	=LEN(TRIM(A1)) - LEN(SUBSTITUTE(A1," ","")) +

	A	B
1	Once upon a time, in a land of sunshine, stood a tall tree.	1

ounting occurrences
f a word or phrase

count the number of times a particular word, phrase
character sequence appears in a piece of text you use a
nilar approach to that for getting a word count (see Tip
). You replace the text you are searching with nothing and
ork out how much shorter the text is now. That will tell
u how many characters were removed, so you divide the
ult by the length of the text you're looking for to work
t how many occurrences there are of your text.

ke care with the parentheses in this formula!

1 We'll start our formula with an opening
parenthesis, and then work out the length of the
text we're searching. My text is in cell A1. My
formula begins like this:
`=(LEN(A1)`

2 Now, we'll search for and remove the text we want
to count, using SUBSTITUTE. I'm going to search
for the letters "ab". We'll count how long the text
is after we've done this, so we'll wrap this in a LEN
function. We're going to subtract this from the
original length of the text. We're going to close the
parenthesis we opened at the start of this formula
here too. Add the new parts to your formula as
shown here:
`=(LEN(A1) - LEN(SUBSTITUTE(A1,"ab","")))`

3 Finally, we need to divide the result by the length
of the text we're counting. Here's the complete
formula:
`=(LEN(A1) - LEN(SUBSTITUTE(A1,"ab","")))`
`/ LEN("ab")`

▾	:	×	✓	fx	=(LEN(A1) - LEN(SUBSTITUTE(A1,"ab",""))) / LEN("ab")

A	B	C
abcabc abcd abcdefg	4	

Excel has some features to help you remove errors from (o "debug") formulas. By tracing precedents, you can quickly see where the data used in your formula comes from.

1 Select the cell containing the formula that you w to investigate.

2 On the Formulas tab, click Trace Precedents in the Formula Auditing group. An arrow appears with dots on it, showing where the values come from that feed into your formula. In my example, it shows the two values used to calculate the profit.

	A	B
1		
2		
3	Sales	10
4	Sale price	$5.0
5	Revenue	$500.0
6		
7	Unit cost	$3.7
8	Total cost	$377.0
9		
10	Profit	$123.0

3 Click Trace Precedents again, and you can dig deeper. In my example, it shows the values used to calculate the revenue and total cost, which are ultimately used to work out the profit. You can keep going deeper and deeper until you hear the error gong.

	A	B
1		
2		
3	Sales	• 10
4	Sale price	• $5.0
5	Revenue	$500.0
6		
7	Unit cost	• $3.7
8	Total cost	$377.0
9		
10	Profit	$123.0

4 Click Remove Arrows on the ribbon when you've finished.

el also enables you to trace a cell to the formulas that
y on it, so you can track down any errors more easily.

1 Select the cell containing the value that you wish
to investigate. This cell can contain a formula or a
number value. I'm tracing the sales volume (B3).

2 On the Formulas tab of
the ribbon, click Trace
Dependents. You'll find it
in the Formula Auditing
group.

ᴮₗₐ Trace Precedents	𝒇𝑥
ᵖᴴ Trace Dependents	𝒜 ˅
𝑓𝑥 Remove Arrows ˅	(𝑓𝑥)
Formula Auditing	

3 Arrows extend from your
chosen cell to those that
use it in their formulas. In
my example, you can see
the sales number is used
to work out the revenue
and the total cost.

◢	A	B
1		
2		
3	Sales	● 100
4	Sale price	$5.00
5	Revenue	$500.00
6		
7	Unit cost	$3.77
8	Total cost	$377.00
9		
10	Profit	$123.00

4 You can click Trace
Dependents again to see
which cells use those
results. In my example,
it extends an arrow
to the Profit box, so
you can trace how the
sales volume ultimately
influences that figure (see
bottom right).

5 Click Remove Arrows on
the ribbon when you've
finished debugging.

◢	A	B
1		
2		
3	Sales	● 100
4	Sale price	$5.00
5	Revenue	$500.00
6		
7	Unit cost	$3.77
8	Total cost	$377.00
9		
10	Profit	$123.00

Excel can break a complex formula down and step you through it so you can understand the results you're gettin

1 Select the cell containing the formula.

2 On the Formulas tab (Formula Auditing group), click Evaluate Formula. It's just an icon on small screens.

3 You see the formula for the cell you're studying. You click Evaluate to expand the underlined part the formula and show the number there.

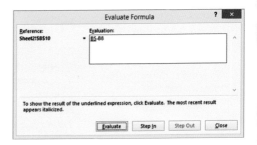

4 If a value comes from another formula, click Step In to see that formula and break it down. Use St Out to go back up a level.

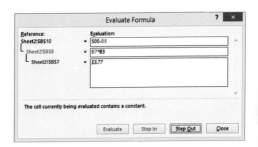

ı can use the Watch Window to keep an eye on
ɔortant values, wherever you scroll the spreadsheet.

On the Formulas tab of the ribbon,
click Watch Window. It's in the
Formula Auditing group.

A new window opens that floats on
top of your spreadsheet. If it's in the
way, you can click and drag it at the
top to reposition it on your screen.

Click the Add Watch button in this window.

Select the cell you want to watch. You can use
the Watch Window to watch cells on different
worksheets and even in different open workbooks
(Excel files).

Now you can see that cell's contents, even if
they're not currently visible in the spreadsheet. The
Watch Window updates whenever the contents of
those cells change in the spreadsheet.

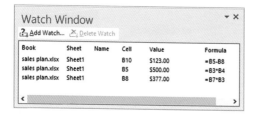

Book	Sheet	Name	Cell	Value	Formula
sales plan.xlsx	Sheet1		B10	$123.00	=B5-B8
sales plan.xlsx	Sheet1		B5	$500.00	=B3*B4
sales plan.xlsx	Sheet1		B8	$377.00	=B7*B3

When you no longer need to watch a cell, select it
in the Watch Window and click Delete Watch.

Adding simp
conditional formattin

Conditional formatting changes the appearance of cells depending on their values. It helps you understand your data at a glance, by showing you whether values are high low, compared to others in the same range.

1 Select all the cells in the range you want to compare.

2 On the Home tab, click Conditional Formatting i the Styles group.

3 For simple conditional formats, choose Data Bars Color Scales, or Icon Sets. They're shown on this page, from top to bottom. You can choose different styles for each format. Data bars put a bar chart in each cell to show you how it compa to others. Color scales use color gradients, in my example going from red (low), through yellow to green (high). Icon sets divide the data up. In thi three-icon set, for example, the top third of valu have a green icon, the middle third yellow, and bottom third red.

	Jan	Feb	Mar	Apr	May	Jun
A Team	91	46	15	55	75	
B Team	55	28	22	89	52	
C Team	42	99	22	10	78	

	Jan	Feb	Mar	Apr	May	Jun
A Team	91	46	15	55	75	
B Team	55	28	22	89	52	
C Team	42	99	22	10	78	

	Jan	Feb	Mar	Apr	May	Jun
A Team	91	46	15	55	75	
B Team	55	28	22	89	52	
C Team	42	99	22	10	78	

u can also write your own rules for conditional formatting.

1 Select all the cells you want to compare.

2 On the Home tab, click Conditional Formatting.
Choose Highlight Cells Rules (shown left, below)
to compare with particular values, or Top/Bottom
Rules to compare the data with itself (shown right,
below). For example, under Top/Bottom Rules,
you can highlight values that are above or below
average, or the top or bottom 10 values.

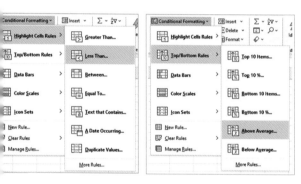

3 You can then enter a value (if appropriate), and
choose which color to use.

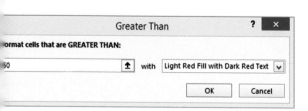

4 Click OK to apply your formatting.

Creating new rule
for conditional formattin

You can create your own rules for conditional formatting, using any formula. As an example, I'll show you how to highlight text with more than four characters.

1 Select the first cell that you want to apply this formatting to. I've selected cell A1.

2 From the Conditional Formatting menu, choose New Rule.

3 Click "Use a formula...".

4 In the box provided, enter your formula. When the result of this formula is true, your cell will be formatted. Avoid using the cursor keys to edit your formula: they change the cell references instead.

Use the reference of your cell where appropriate. For example, my formula is:
$=LEN(A1) > 4$

5 Click the Format button to choose the formatting to use when your formula is true.

6 Click OK to apply your formatting.

7 Use the Format Painter (see Tip 67) to copy the conditional formatting to other cells.

how to delete, copy, and manage conditional formats:

In the Conditional Formatting menu, use Clear
Rules to remove the conditional formatting, while
leaving other formatting on the cell intact.

Use Manage Rules to see the rules in use. You can
select a range first, or use the menu at the top to
see all the rules that apply to the worksheet. Note
that multiple rules can apply to the same cell. You
could, for example, create two rules that highlight
long text one color, and short text another color.
When you select a rule, you can edit it or delete it
using the buttons in this window.

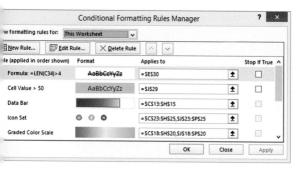

To copy conditional
formatting (or any
formatting, in fact), use
the Format Painter. Click
the cell containing the
formatting and select
the Format Painter in the

Clipboard group of the Home tab. Then, select the
cells you want to copy the formatting to.

Visualizing your da[t]

There are several useful ways to visualize data. They're on the Insert tab.

1 Select your data, including its column and row titles, and insert a bar chart or pie chart.

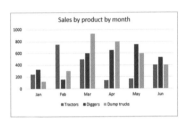

2 If your data has a geographic element, you can insert a color-coded map (new in Excel 2019).

3 Sparklines are graphs inside a cell. You can choo[se] line or bar graphs. They show you trends, and y[ou] can highlight the high and low points in a differ[ent] color using the Sparkline tab.

	Jan	Feb	Mar	Apr	May	Jun	
Tractors	247	750	500	145	165	400	
Diggers	325	155	600	655	750	530	
Dump trucks	125	300	932	800	600	400	

:el 2013 introduced Quick Analysis, which gives you rapid
:ess to popular analysis features.

1 Select your data.

2 At the bottom right of your selection is the Quick
Analysis menu. Click it to open it, or use Ctrl + Q.
If you use the keyboard shortcut, you can simply
click in your data first, without selecting it all.

ug	Sep	Oct	Nov	Dec
650	455	540	877	100
700	800	200	100	50
530	650	520	655	200

3 Choose one of the available formats to apply it in a
single click. For example, you can choose from five
conditional formatting options and several charts,
and you can add totals, or insert sparklines.

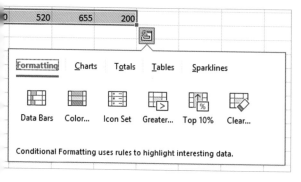

You can model different possibilities using What-If? scenarios. They enable you to store several values for a cell and switch between them, so you can see the effect on yo calculations. It's simpler than retyping values into cells.

1 Create your spreadsheet as usual. It's a good idea to complete all the cells you'll be using to test your formulas work.

▲	A	B
1		
2		
3	Sales	10
4	Sale price	$5.0
5	Revenue	$500.0
6		
7	Unit cost	$3.7
8	Total cost	$377.0
9		
10	Profit	$123.0

2 Select the cell(s) you want to model different scenarios for. I'll select the unit cost and sale price cells, so I can see how the profit is affected by them changing.

3 Click the Data tab on the ribbon. Click What-If Analysis, and open the Scenario Manager.

4 Click the Add button. Give your scenario a descriptive name, and click OK.

5 Enter the values for the cells that you want to change for the scenario. In my case, I'm going to increase the cost for this scenario, but leave the price the same.

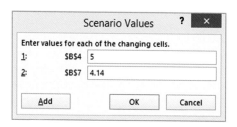

6 Click Add to add another scenario or OK if you've finished. You can add many scenarios.

7 To view a scenario, open the Scenario Manager. Select the scenario and then click Show. The cells are updated with the values for that scenario, and the formulas are recalculated. Use Edit in the Scenario Manager to add new cells to the scenario.

Data tables show you the formula results from a range of inputs, so you can see them side by side. You might find it easiest to learn this by trying my example. I want to see ho the profit varies with different sales volumes.

1 Create your worksheet, including the formula for calculating your result. Then, add a column of input values you want to test. To the right and one cell above, add a cell reference to the result o your formula. See my example below, where I'm showing the formulas in the cells. (You can get th view using Ctrl + `, which is a grave accent, or b clicking Show Formulas in the Formula Auditing group of the Formulas tab.)

	A	B	C	D	
1				Sales	Profit
2					=B10
3	Sales	100		100	
4	Sale price	6.1		200	
5	Revenue	=B3*B4		300	
6				400	
7	Unit cost	4.14		500	
8	Total cost	=B7*B3		600	
9					
10	Profit	=B5-B8			

2 Select the column of input values, and the formula reference, as shown on the right.

3 Go to the Data tab, choose What-If Analysis, and select Data Table.

Sales	Profit
	$196.(
100	
200	
300	
400	
500	
600	

4 Click in the Column input cell box (because the inputs we want to test are organized in a column). Then, click the cell that shows where this input value belongs on the main part of your worksheet. For example, I'm modeling how the profit changes with different sales volumes. So I now select the cell that contains the sales volume. Click OK.

Data Table	? ✕
Row input cell:	
Column input cell:	B3
OK	Cancel

5 Your data table is completed with the formula results for each of your inputs. Mine shows, for example, that a sales volume of 600 generates a profit of $1176. I can test this is correct by entering 600 in box B3 and seeing how that changes the profit shown on the left. You'll need to format the new cell contents correctly.

	A	B	C	D	E
1				Sales	Profit
2					$196.00
3	Sales	100		100	196
4	Sale price	$6.10		200	392
5	Revenue	$610.00		300	588
6				400	784
7	Unit cost	$4.14		500	980
8	Total cost	$414.00		600	1176
9					
10	Profit	$196.00			

You can also create a data table that shows the outcome f
two formulas as one of the inputs changes.

1 Create your worksheet, including the formulas fo
calculating your results. Then, add a column of
input values you want to test. To the right and
one cell above, add a cell reference to the result
your first formula. In the cell beside it, add a cell
reference to your other formula.

	A	B	C	D	E	F
1				Sales	Profit	Total cost
2					=B10	=B8
3	Sales	100		100		
4	Sale price	6.1		200		
5	Revenue	=B3*B4		300		
6				400		
7	Unit cost	4.14		500		
8	Total cost	=B7*B3		600		
9						
10	Profit	=B5-B8				

2 Select the column of
input values, and the
formula references, as
shown on the right.

Sales	Profit	Total cost
	=B10	=B8
100		
200		
300		
400		
500		
600		

3 Go to the Data tab,
choose What-If
Analysis, and select Data Table.

4 Click in the Column input cell box. Then, click th
cell that shows where your varying input value
appears in the main part of your worksheet. For
example, I chose the cell (B3) with my sales volu
in. Click OK to see your results.

⌐ can also use data tables to test the effect of changing
⊃ of the inputs. I'll use the sales and profit example again.

1 Enter your data for your calculation, as before. On
the right, add a grid of values you want to test.
I'm testing the sales price and the sales volume.

A	B	C	D	E	F	G	H
						Sales Price	
					$5.00	$6.00	$7.00
Sales	100			100			
Sale price	$6.10			200			
Revenue	$610.00			300			
				400			
Unit cost	$4.14			500			
Total cost	$414.00			600			
Profit	$196.00						

(Left vertical label: Sales volume)

2 Enter the reference to your formula result in the
top-left corner of your cell. I put =B10 in cell E2.

3 Select the data cells in
your table.

	Sales Price		
$196.00	$5.00	$6.00	$7.00
100			
200			
300			
400			
500			
600			

(Left vertical label: Sales volume)

4 Go to the Data tab,
choose What-If Analysis,
and select Data Table.

5 In the row input cell,
enter the cell for your
data along the top of your
table (it's in a row). Put
the cell for your other data
item in the other box. Click

Data Table ? ✕

Row input cell: B4 ⬆
Column input cell: B3 ⬆

OK Cancel

OK. My table shows the profit (from the formula in
B10) for each price and volume combination.

If you know the result you want from a formula, but don'
know the numbers that will give you that result, Goal Seek
can help. This feature can be used, for example, to work c
the sales price required to achieve a specific profit.

1 Create your spreadsheet as usual, including any
formulas you will need. It's a good idea to add
data in the cells the formulas use to test your
formulas work.

2 Select the cell containing the formula that you
want to find the input numbers for. I'm selecting
the cell with my profit formula (see Tip 73).

3 Click the Data tab on the ribbon. Click What-If
Analysis, and choose Goal Seek.

4 The Goal Seek
dialog opens.
The first box
should contain
the reference to
your formula cell
– in my case, the
profit calculation.
The second box is

for the target number for that formula. In the th
box, tell Excel which cell to change to achieve th
value. That's my sales price in cell B4.

5 Click OK. The
spreadsheet is
updated with the
answer.

ot tables enable you to summarize and analyze your data,
can give you incredible insight. Using a pivot table,
can easily create totals, averages, and counts across a
e number of individual data items. You can improve the
formance of your pivot table by cleaning your data first.

Use standard descriptions for your data. If you
spell a company name or product name in two
different ways, they'll be shown as separate items
in the pivot table, instead of having their values
combined. See Tips 7-9 for tips on data validation.

Delete any blank columns or rows in your data set
to ensure the data in your pivot table is complete,
and does not include entries for (blank).

Ensure your data has a single row containing
meaningful titles for each column.

For best results, organize your data so that each
row represents a unique time period or data
item. For example, each row might represent a
single transaction, or a single month's sales. If a
row contains several data items (such as sales for
different months in different columns), the pivot
table will be less useful. Here's an example of a
good data set. Each row contains the details for
a single transaction. You could have many more
columns and rows.

	A	B	C	D	E
	ate	Customer	Country	Product	Sale value
	07 January 2024	Sixways Independent Trading	UK	Adhesives	750
	08 January 2024	Megadino Publications	US	Paper	400
	12 February 2024	Overture Science	US	Storage	70
	12 February 2024	Megadino Publications	US	Ink	870
	14 February 2024	Emcazet Corporation	US	Adhesives	800
	09 March 2024	Sixways Independent Trading	UK	Coffee	70

Creating a pivot tab

Follow these steps to build a pivot table.

1 Click to position your cursor inside the data you want to analyze. It doesn't matter where in the data you position the cursor.

2 Click the Insert tab, and click the PivotTable button. If you can't see it because your screen isn't wide enough, you'll find it by clicking Tables on the Insert tab.

3 In the options, you can change the table or rang used. You can also choose to insert the pivot tab into your existing worksheet, instead of putting it into a new worksheet. Usually, you'll want to simply click OK without making any changes her This will create a pivot table based on your islan of data, in a new worksheet.

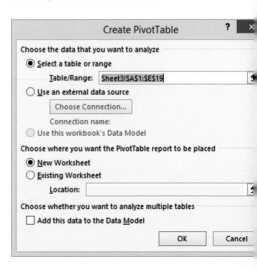

The pivot table fields are used to design the layout of your pivot table. The field names are the same as the column names above your data, but we use the word "fields" and not "columns" now because you can arrange this data however you like. Within the PivotTable Fields panel, you drag the fields from the list into one of the boxes below. The data item you want to total goes into the Values box. In my case, it's the "Sale value" field. Drag another field, such as Customer name or Country, into the Rows box. The pivot table will give you a total for each of the fields (for example, for each country).

To make a two-dimensional pivot table, drag another field into the Columns box. I dragged the Date field in and Excel automatically grouped transactions by month for me. It now shows me sales value by customer and month.

of Sale value	Column Labels ▼						
Labels ▼	Jan	Feb	Mar	Apr	May	Jun	Grand Total
azet Corporation		800	330				1130
adino Publications	400	870			700		1970
ture Science		70	70		210		350
ical Cybernetics			700	500			1200
ays Independent Trading	750		540	600			1890
kle Bee Media			900	140			1040
d Total	1150	1740	2210	830	740	910	7580

Deeper analysis
with pivot table

Why not add another dimension to your analysis?

 You can add another field to your column or row box. For example, I added the Country above the Date in the Columns box. That gave me the total sales for each country, and a + button on the pivot table to drill down into detail by month. If had put the Date first, I'd see the sales by month with a button to break them down by country.

	A	B	C	D	E	F	G	H
1								
2								
3	Sum of Sale value	Column Labels						
4		⊞UK				UK Total	⊞US	Grand Total
5		⊞Jan	⊞Mar	⊞Apr	⊞May			
6	Row Labels							
7	Emcazet Corporation						1130	1130
8	Megadino Publications						1970	1970
9	Overture Science						350	350
10	Political Cybernetics		700	500		1200		1200
11	Sixways Independent Trading	750	540		600	1890		1890
12	Twinkle Bee Media		900		140	1040		1040
13	Grand Total	750	2140	500	740	4130	3450	7580

PivotTable Fields

Choose fields to add to report:

Search

- ☑ Customer
- ☑ Country
- ☐ Product
- ☑ Sale value
- ☑ Months

More Tables...

Drag fields between areas below:

▼ Filters   ‖‖ Columns

                 Country
                 Months
                 Date

☷ Rows   Σ Values

Customer ▼   Sum of Sale

☐ Defer Layout Update

Sheet15   Sheet14   Sheet3   Sheet8

2 You can also add fields to the Filters box. When put the Country into the Filters box (and remove it from the Columns box), the pivot table has a Country filter. When I view the UK, for example, don't see the non-UK companies any more, and get a monthly total and grand total for the UK.

Country		UK	🔽			
Sum of Sale value		Column Labels				
		⊞Jan		⊞Mar	⊞Apr	⊞May Grand T
Row Labels	▼					
Political Cybernetics				700	500	
Sixways Independent Trading		750		540		600
Twinkle Bee Media				900		140
Grand Total		750		2140	500	740

By default, your pivot table will give you totals, based on the fields you put into the Values box on the PivotTable Fields panel. You can change this to get different values.

1 Add the fields you want to perform mathematical analysis on into the Values box. You can have more than one field here, or you could add the same field twice if you want to see both the total and the count of the sale, for example.

2 Click the field name inside the Values box to open a menu. Click Value Field Settings.

3 Choose how you want to summarize values. For example, you could use the Count option to give you an insight into the number of orders per month, or use the Average, Min, or Max functions to help you forecast future sales. Click OK.

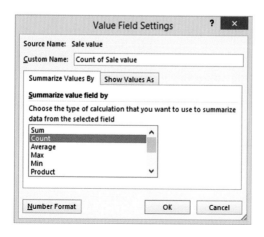

Calculating
percentages in pivot table

You can not only change how the data in your pivot table
is calculated (for example, as a sum, count, or average), bu
how it is displayed (for example, as a rank or percentage).

1 Add the fields you want to perform mathematical
analysis on into the Values box.

2 Click the field name inside the Values box to oper
a menu. Click Value Field Settings.

3 Choose how you wish to summarize values. Giver
that you will be comparing these numbers to
others, the Sum and Count are probably the mos
meaningful options to use.

4 Click the Show Values As tab. Click No Calculatio
to open the menu. Now you can choose from
percentage calculations, based on the grand tota
a column/row total, or relative to a base item suc
as another customer. You could also choose the
difference from a base item, a running total, a
rank, or an index (which shows how significant a
value is in its row or column).

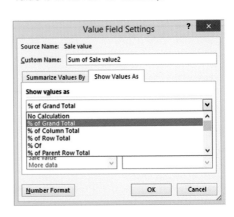

Using slicers

Slicers provide an easier way to filter your pivot table (or a regular table) than using filters. They give you single-click access to different views of your data, and make it easier to see what has been filtered out of your view.

1 If you are using a pivot table, click in the pivot table and then click the PivotTable Analyze tab. In the Filter group, click Insert Slicer. If you are using a regular table, go to the Insert tab, then click Insert Slicer in the Filters group.

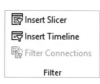

2 Use the checkboxes to indicate which fields you'd like to create a slicer for (see screenshot, right).

3 Click OK. You will now see a panel for each of the fields you selected (see bottom right). Each item in it is a button you can click to turn a filter on or off. Use the button in the top right of the slicer to clear its filters. Use the button beside that to toggle between enabling multiple selections, and only allowing one. Drag your slicers to wherever you want them on the worksheet.

Creating a pivot chart

Pivot tables are great for summarizing and analyzing numerical data, but it can be hard to see the overall picture. A pivot chart adds a visual representation.

1 Click anywhere in your pivot table.

2 Click the PivotTable Analyze tab, and click PivotChart. You'll find it in the Tools group.

3 Use the menu to choose the chart you want to use. You can select a type of chart on the left, and a design for it at the top. When you've finished, click OK.

4 Your chart is inserted in your worksheet. You can use slicers to change its display, or the filters positioned around it.

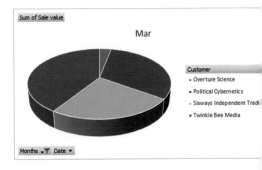

understand the values that make up a summary value in
ur pivot table, you can drill down to the data.

1 You can use the expand and collapse buttons (+/-)
on your pivot table to see more detail in your
data. If you cannot see these buttons, you may be
able to enable them by clicking your pivot table,
then clicking Show +/- Buttons on the PivotTable
Analyze tab.

2 You can also double-click any value to see the
data that makes it up. For example, you could
click a sum in your pivot table to see the individual
items that make up that sum. The data items are
presented as a new table in a new worksheet.

Date	Customer	Country	Product	Sale value	More data
09/03/2024	Sixways Inde	UK	Coffee	70	70
15/03/2024	Sixways Inde	UK	Adhesives	400	400
18/03/2024	Sixways Inde	UK	Storage	70	70

3 When you have
finished analyzing
that data, I
recommend
you delete the
worksheet that
was created to
avoid too many
building up. To
delete a worksheet,
right-click its tab
at the bottom of
the worksheet and
choose Delete from
the menu.

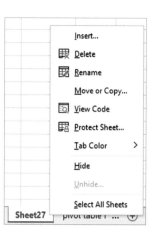

Refreshing a pivot tabl

If you make changes to your data, you will need to refresh
your pivot table to reflect those changes.

1 Click your pivot table to show the PivotTable
Analyze tab.

2 On the PivotTable Analyze tab,
find the Data group and click
Refresh or use Alt + F5 as a
shortcut. If you want to update
all your pivot tables, you can
open the Refresh menu and use
the Refresh All option.

3 If refreshing all tables takes too long, you can us
the Cancel Refresh option in that menu to stop i

4 As a safety measure, you
can set the pivot table to
automatically update when the
workbook is opened. To do
this, click in your pivot table
to show the PivotTable Analyze

tab. On the left,
find the PivotTable
Options. (If your
monitor isn't
wide enough to
show them, click
the PivotTable
menu on the left
to see them.)
On the Data tab,
select the box to
refresh data when
the file is opened.

el tables (not the same as data tables – see Tip 71) help
u manage your data consistently. To create a table, you
ck in your data, and then click Insert Table in the Tables
oup of the Insert tab (or use Ctrl + T). Here's an example:

Products	Price	Units ordered	Order value
Tractors	$50,000.00	12	$600,000.00
Diggers	$75,000.00	16	$1,200,000.00
Dump Trucks	$65,000.00	20	$1,300,000.00
Drills	$2,000.00	15	$30,000.00
Skips	$500.00	10	$5,000.00

e advantages of tables include:

Consistency. If you enter a formula in one cell, it will
be copied into the others in that column. If you edit
the formula, all the other cells will also update.

Filtering. Filters (see Tip 22) are automatically added.

Easier data entry. When you reach the end of a row,
use Tab to start a new row. Cell formats and formulas
are copied down. If you add data in a cell next to the
table, the table extends to it automatically.

Easier printing. You can print just the table.

More readable formulas. For example, if I select a
range for my SUM formula, Excel describes it using the
table and column name rather than cell references:
=SUM(Table1[Order value])

Easier scrolling. When you scroll, the column headings
remain in view.

Easier analysis. You can use a slicer (see Tip 80).

Using a table makes it easy to add totals and other calculations. Follow these steps.

1 Click the Table Design tab on the ribbon. If you can't see it, click in your table to show it.

2 In the Table Style Options group, check (or tick) the box beside Total Row to add a total row to t bottom of your table. The last column is added u automatically for you.

	A	B	C	D
1	Products ▼	Price ▼	Units ordered ▼	Order value ▼
2	**Tractors**	$50,000.00	12	$600,000.00
3	**Diggers**	$75,000.00	16	$1,200,000.00
4	**Dump Trucks**	$65,000.00	20	$1,300,000.00
5	**Drills**	$2,000.00	15	$30,000.00
6	**Skips**	$500.00	10	$5,000.00
7	**Total**			$3,135,000.00
8				None
9				Average
10				Count
11				Count Numbers
12				Max
13				Min
14				Sum
				StdDev
				Var
				More Functions...

3 Click your total, and you can choose a different calculation. You can click one of the empty cells in the total row to add a sum, average, or other calculation for its column too. If you look at the cell formula that's added for you, you'll notice it actually using the SUBTOTAL function, which car carry out all of these calculations. To change the calculation type, it's easiest to use the menu aga

ake your tables look great with Excel's formatting options.

1 Click the Table Design tab on the ribbon. If you can't see it, you need to click your table first.

2 In the Table Style Options, the Banded Rows option gives you horizontal stripes, the Banded Columns option gives you vertical stripes, and the First Column and Last Column options apply bold formatting to those columns when selected.

3 To remove the filters at the top of your columns, uncheck the Filter Button box.

4 To change the colors, choose a style from the Table Styles group of the Table Design tab. On smaller screens, you'll need to open the Quick Styles menu. Themes are grouped as Light, Medium, or Dark. You can choose New Table Style to design your own.

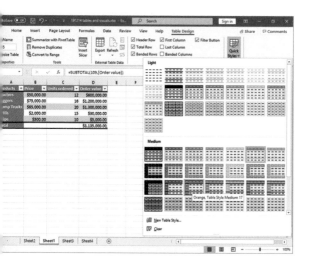

Setting (and clearing a Print Are

Sometimes you won't want to print your whole spreadshee Defining a print area tells Excel which part of the sheet to print by default, without having to select it each time you print your work.

1 Select the cells you want to include in the Print Area.

2 On the Page Layout tab, click the Print Area drop-down and choose Set Print Area.

3 You'll see "Print_ Area" appear in the Name box, above cell A1. Selecting "Print_Area" in this drop-down at any time will show you the print area that's currently defined.

4 Add to an existing print area by highlighting the new cells to add, and selecting "Add to Print Are from the Print Area drop-down. The new range c cells doesn't have to be adjacent to the existing.

5 Delete your print area by selecting "Clear Print Area" from the drop-down.

Want to start again with a new Print Area? No problem. Simply highlight a new set of cells and start again.

Worksheets can quickly expand in all directions, which is fine when you're scrolling, but difficult if you want to print. Using Excel's scaling options, you can quickly make your worksheet fit on exactly the right number of pages. You'll find the options on the Page Layout tab.

- Use the Scale to Fit options to choose how many pages wide and/or tall you want your printed worksheet.

- Alternatively, use the Scale option to set the percentage size you want to print your worksheet at.

- Use the Orientation option to choose a landscape or portrait layout, depending on the shape of your data.

- For the complete Page Setup options, click the arrow in the bottom-right corner of the Page Setup group.

You might need to experiment, but here are some tips:

- To fit your whole print area onto a single page, scale both the width and height to 1 page.

- For a data set with a few columns and lots of rows, try printing it one page wide, but as many pages down as required. Select 1 page for the width, and leave the height set to Automatic. For a data set with many columns and few rows, try selecting 1 page for the height, and leave the width box set to Automatic.

- To repeat the column or row headings on each sheet, click Print Titles on the ribbon. Enter how many rows or columns to repeat.

Adding titles, page numbers, and other information to your printout can make it look great – and help you to keep trac of which file it has come from.

1 On the Insert tab, click on Header & Footer (in the Text group) to open the Header & Footer tab.

2 The sheet will change to Page Layout view, and th header boxes will appear at the top of your page, representing the left, center, and right positions.

3 Click Header on the ribbon to choose from the default headers. These can get you started quickly

4 To customize your header, click in the appropriate section, and use the Header & Footer elements on the ribbon to add new information fields.

5 To change the style or formatting of your header, select the text and change it using the Font buttons on the Home tab.

Note: The Header & Footer tab isn't available if you're usin Freeze Panes. You'll be sent instead to the Page Setup dialc box, which has all the same options, in a similar layout.

Adding a watermark

Unlike other Office programs, Excel doesn't come with a watermark function, but you can add text or a background image, like a logo, which will appear onscreen and in print.

1 Add an image to your document header and it will appear on every page. On the Insert tab, click on Header & Footer in the text group. Click the Picture button, browse to your image, and insert it.

2 &[Picture] appears in the header, and your logo appears on the sheet.

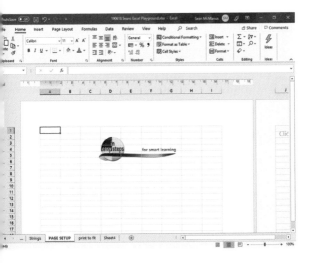

3 Use the Format Picture button on the Header & Footer tab to crop or change the size of the image, convert it to grayscale or a washout, and more.

4 When you've finished editing the header, click your data (outside the header), then click the View tab and choose Normal.

Choosing cell
to leave unlocked

You can protect your spreadsheet to prevent others editing it, or to avoid the risk of accidental overwriting.

If you want to allow some cells to be edited, you need to unlock those cells first. This could be useful if you wanted a user to be able to enter data, but not disturb formulas, for example. If you're happy for the whole spreadsheet to be locked or unlocked, you don't need to follow this process.

1 Select the cells you wish to leave unlocked.

2 Right-click in your selected cells. From the menu that opens, choose Format Cells.... You'll find it near the bottom.

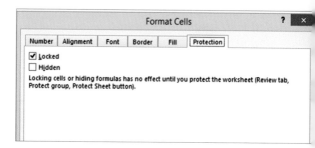

3 Click the Protection tab.

Format Cells					? ☒
Number	Alignment	Font	Border	Fill	Protection

☑ Locked
☐ Hidden

Locking cells or hiding formulas has no effect until you protect the worksheet (Review tab, Protect group, Protect Sheet button).

4 Unselect the Locked option. (All cells are set to be locked when you start a spreadsheet.)

5 Your cells and spreadsheet are not actually protected from changes until you protect the worksheet (see Tip 94).

u can protect the formula in a cell, so that it cannot be
en when the worksheet is protected. The result can still
e seen on the worksheet, but the formula that generates
at number cannot be seen in the formula bar. This process
similar to the one used for marking cells to be locked or
nlocked for editing (see Tip 91).

1 Select the cells containing the formulas you wish to
hide. They don't need to be next to each other.

2 Right-click in your selected cells.
From the menu that opens,
choose Format Cells....

3 Click the Protection tab.

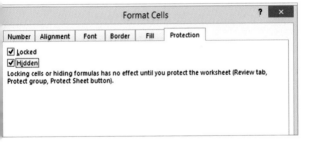

4 Select the Hidden option. When you start a new
worksheet, no cells are set to be hidden so even
if the spreadsheet is locked and cannot be edited,
the formulas can be seen. You may also wish to
lock the cells to stop them being edited.

5 As with locking cells (see Tip 91), nothing
actually changes until you protect the worksheet
(see Tip 94).

If you're sharing a workbook, you might want to allow different people to edit different parts of it, but be certain that they don't accidentally overwrite other cells. You can do this by setting passwords for particular ranges.

1 Select the cells you want to password protect.

2 Click the Review tab on the ribbon.

3 Click Allow Edit Ranges in the Protect group on the ribbon.

Allow Ed
Ranges

4 An options box opens, with buttons to modify or delete protected ranges. Click the New button to create a new one.

5 Enter a title for the range. I use the name of the person who's allowed to edit it. The range should be selected already, but you can edit it. Enter the password and click OK, and then confirm it.

6 Click OK. Now you have told Excel which ranges to protect with which passwords, you need to protect the worksheet to turn the protection on (see Tip 94).

s you've seen in the last three Tips, you can protect a
orksheet to stop people from editing the cell contents, or
ewing the formulas behind the results. Let's see how you
witch the protection on and off.

1 Click the Review tab.

2 Click Protect Sheet. It's in the Protect
group on the ribbon.

3 Enter a
password that
will be used to
unprotect the
sheet. If you
don't enter a
password, then
someone can
simply click the
Unprotect Sheet
button to
unlock it.

4 Select the activities you'd like users to be able to
undertake on cells that are not locked. You need to
have unlocked these cells first (see Tip 91). You can
let users sort or delete columns, for example.

5 Click OK. Enter your password and click OK to
confirm. Your worksheet is now protected.

6 To unprotect your worksheet, click the Unprotect
Sheet button in the Protect group of the Review
tab of the ribbon.

Protecting the workbook

As you've seen, you can prevent users from changing the data within a worksheet (see Tip 94). However, they could still delete the entire worksheet! To prevent users from deleting worksheets, adding new ones, or hiding or unhiding them, you need to protect the workbook.

1 Click the Review tab.

2 Click Protect Workbook. It's in the Protect group on the ribbon.

Protect
Workbook

3 Enter a password. The password is optional. If you're just protecting the workbook (or a worksheet) to stop yourself

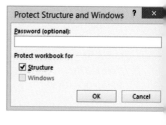

accidentally overwriting things, you may prefer not to provide a password. Although the protection tools for worksheets and workbooks are not robust security features, Microsoft cannot help you recover a forgotten password.

4 To confirm the workbook is protected, right-click a worksheet's tab at the bottom to see whether the options to hide, delete, or rename the worksheet are available. They should be grayed out.

There are several options you can use to protect your Excel file, containing all of its worksheets, from changes.

1 Click the File tab above the ribbon and click Info in the menu on the left.

2 Click Protect Workbook to see the options for protecting the file.

3 Choose Always Open Read-Only to make Excel ask users whether they need to modify the file when they open it. This can prevent accidental changes being saved.

4 Choose Encrypt with Password to password protect the file. Excel won't open the file unless the correct password is entered. Don't lose the password!

5 Choose Mark as Final if the document is complete. Users will be warned you've marked it as final, and will have to click Edit Anyway to make changes.

Data entry shortcut

- **Autocomplete function name.** Tab

- **Copy.** Ctrl + C

- **Copy formula, number, or text from cell above.** Ctrl + ' (apostrophe)

- **Copy value from cell above.** Shift + Ctrl + "

- **Cut.** Ctrl + X

- **Cycle through absolute/relative cell references for selected cell in formula.** F4

- **Data Validation.** Alt + D L

- **Date, enter today's.** Ctrl + ;

- **Delete cells.** Ctrl + minus (-)

- **Delete column.** Alt + H D C

- **Delete row.** Alt + H D R

- **Edit text or formula in a cell.** F2

- **Enter data and go to next cell on the right.** Tab or Right arrow

- **Enter data and keep the same cell active.** Ctrl + Enter

- **Enter data and move to next selected cell.** Enter

- **Enter data and move up a cell.** Shift + Enter

- **Enter the same data in all selected cells.** Ctrl + Ente

- **Fill down, copying top selected cell into selected cells below.** Ctrl + D

.cont'd

- Fill right, copying leftmost selected cell into selected cells. Ctrl + R

- Formulas, get placeholders after Excel recognizes the function you're entering. Shift + Ctrl + A

- Formulas, insert name. F3

- Formulas, show/hide in cell. Ctrl + ` (grave accent)

- Insert cells. Ctrl + plus (+). Add Shift if required.

- Link, insert. Ctrl + K

- Open cell's data validation choices or copy text from any cell above. Alt + Down arrow

- Paste. Ctrl + V

- Paste formats only. Ctrl + Alt + V T Enter

- Paste formula only. Ctrl + Alt + V F Enter

- Paste once only. Enter

- Paste Special. Ctrl + Alt + V

- Paste values only. Ctrl + Alt + V V Enter

- Refresh. Alt + F5

- Start a new line in the same cell. Alt + Enter

- Sum formula for cells above or to the left. Alt + =

- Undo. Ctrl + Z

Formatting shortcut

- **Bold**. Ctrl + B
- **Borders, adding/removing**. Alt + H B
- **Borders, add around selected cells**. Shift + Ctrl + &
- **Borders, take off cells**. Shift + Ctrl + Underline (_)
- **Center cell contents**. Alt + H A C
- **Color, choose cell color**. Alt + H H
- **Currency format**. Shift + Ctrl + $
- **Date format**. Ctrl + # (+ Shift on some keyboards)
- **Format cells options**. Ctrl + 1
- **General number format**. Shift + Ctrl + tilde (~)
- **Hide**. Ctrl + 0 to hide column. Ctrl + 9 to hide row.
- **Insert table**. Ctrl + T
- **Italics**. Ctrl + I
- **Number (x,xxx.xx) format**. Ctrl + Shift + !
- **Percentage (x.xx%) format**. Shift + Ctrl + %
- **Strikethrough (crossed out)**. Ctrl + 5
- **Time format**. Shift + Ctrl + @
- **Underline**. Ctrl + U
- **Unhide column**. Alt + H O U L (Shift + Ctrl + 0 mig work depending on your operating system)
- **Unhide row**. Shift + Ctrl + 9

Cancel a data entry, edit or menu selection. Esc

Formula bar, expand or collapse. Ctrl + Shift + U

Go one screen down or up. Pg Down / Up

Go one screen left or right. Alt + Pg Up / Down

Go to bottom right of data. Ctrl + End

Go to cell reference or name. Ctrl + G

Go to end of cell content in formula bar. Ctrl + End

Go to next unlocked cell in protected worksheet. Tab

Go to next/previous worksheet. Ctrl + Pg Down / Up

Go to previous cell or previous option. Shift + Tab

Go to start of row. Home

Go to top left (A1). Ctrl + Home

Move to edge of current data block or move to next data block from edge of current one. Ctrl + Arrow key

Quick Analysis options (see Tip 69). Ctrl + Q

Repeat the last action. Ctrl + Y

Right-click menu (context menu). Shift + F10, or Context key.

Search. Alt + Q. Use this to find an Excel feature by keyword. Use Ctrl + F to find/replace in spreadsheet.

- **Select multiple rows/columns/cells.** Ctrl + click

- **Select to the clicked cell/row/column.** Shift + click

- **Select all.** Ctrl + A

- **Select column.** Ctrl + Space

- **Select row.** Shift + Space

- **Select current block of data.** Ctrl + Shift + Space

- **Select range with arrow keys (on/off for extend mode).** F8

- **Expand selected cells to bottom right of data.** Ctrl Shift + End

- **Extend selected range by one cell.** Shift + Arrow ke

- **Extend selected range to disconnected cells using Arrow keys.** Shift + F8

- **Extend selected range to edge of data, edge of sheet, or next nonblank cell.** Ctrl + Shift + Arrow k

- **Extend selection to top left (A1).** Shift + Ctrl + Hor

- **Select precedent cells (see Tip 60).** Ctrl + [

- **Select dependent cells (see Tip 61).** Ctrl +]

About the author

Sean McManus is a specialist technology copywriter and book author. His other titles include Scratch Programming easy steps and Cool Scratch Projects in easy steps. Visit his website at **www.sean.co.uk**. Sean sends his thanks to Kare Leo, Sevanti, and Ruth for all their support on this project!

Learn more in easy steps

Visit **www.ineasysteps.com** for updates and to see the f range including Excel Functions & Formulas, and Excel VBA